Themistocles

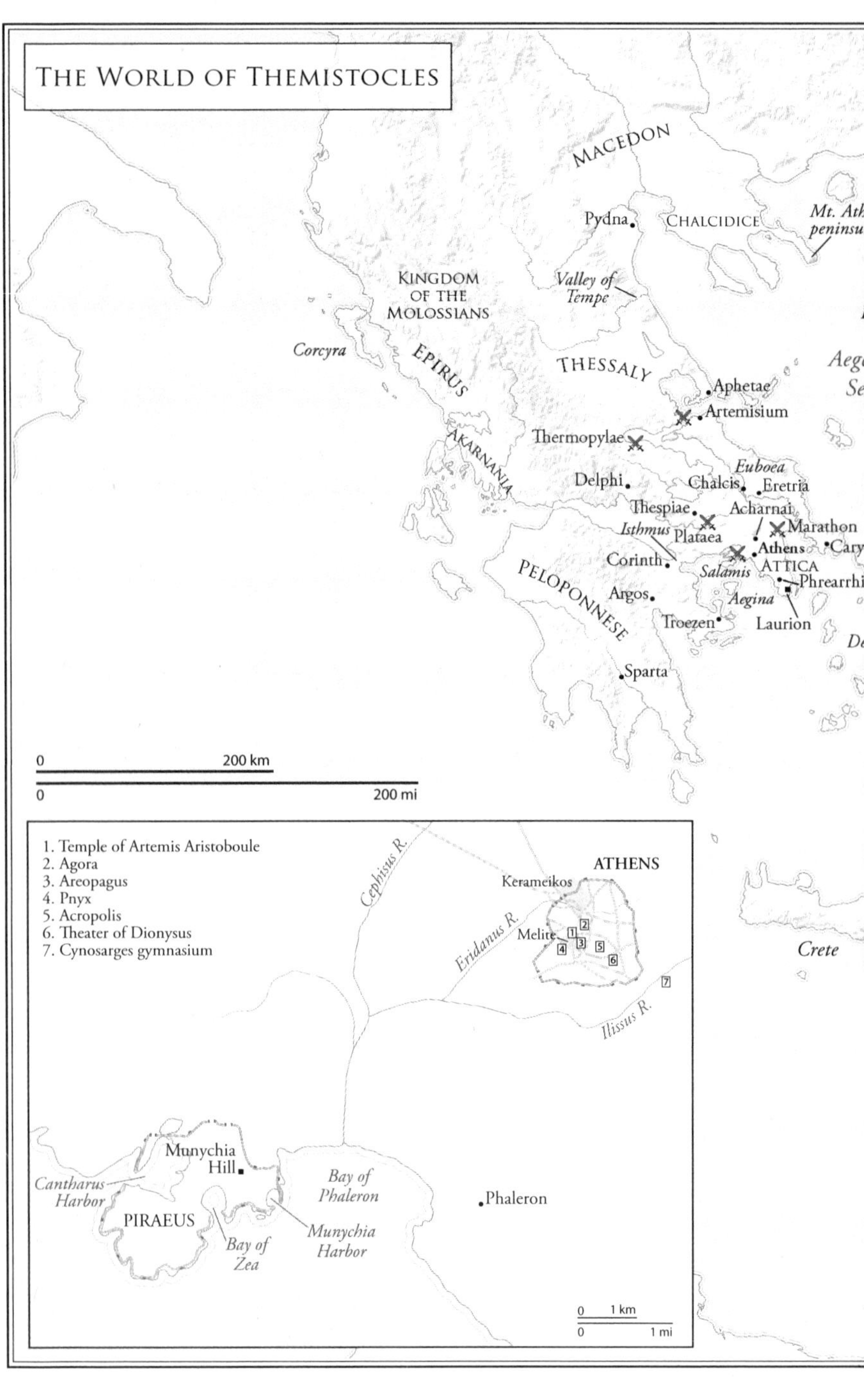
THE WORLD OF THEMISTOCLES
MACEDON
Pydna
CHALCIDICE
Mt. Athos peninsula
KINGDOM OF THE MOLOSSIANS
Valley of Tempe
Corcyra
EPIRUS
THESSALY
Aegean Sea
Aphetae
Artemisium
Thermopylae
AKARNANIA
Euboea
Delphi
Chalcis
Eretria
Thespiae
Acharnai
Isthmus
Plataea
Marathon
Athens
Corinth
Salamis
ATTICA
PELOPONNESE
Phrearrhi
Argos
Aegina
Troezen
Laurion
Sparta
0 200 km
0 200 mi
1. Temple of Artemis Aristoboule
2. Agora
3. Areopagus
4. Pnyx
5. Acropolis
6. Theater of Dionysus
7. Cynosarges gymnasium
Cephisus R.
ATHENS
Kerameikos
Eridanus R.
Melite
Crete
Ilissus R.
Munychia Hill
Cantharus Harbor
Bay of Phaleron
Phaleron
PIRAEUS
Munychia Harbor
Bay of Zea
0 1 km
0 1 mi

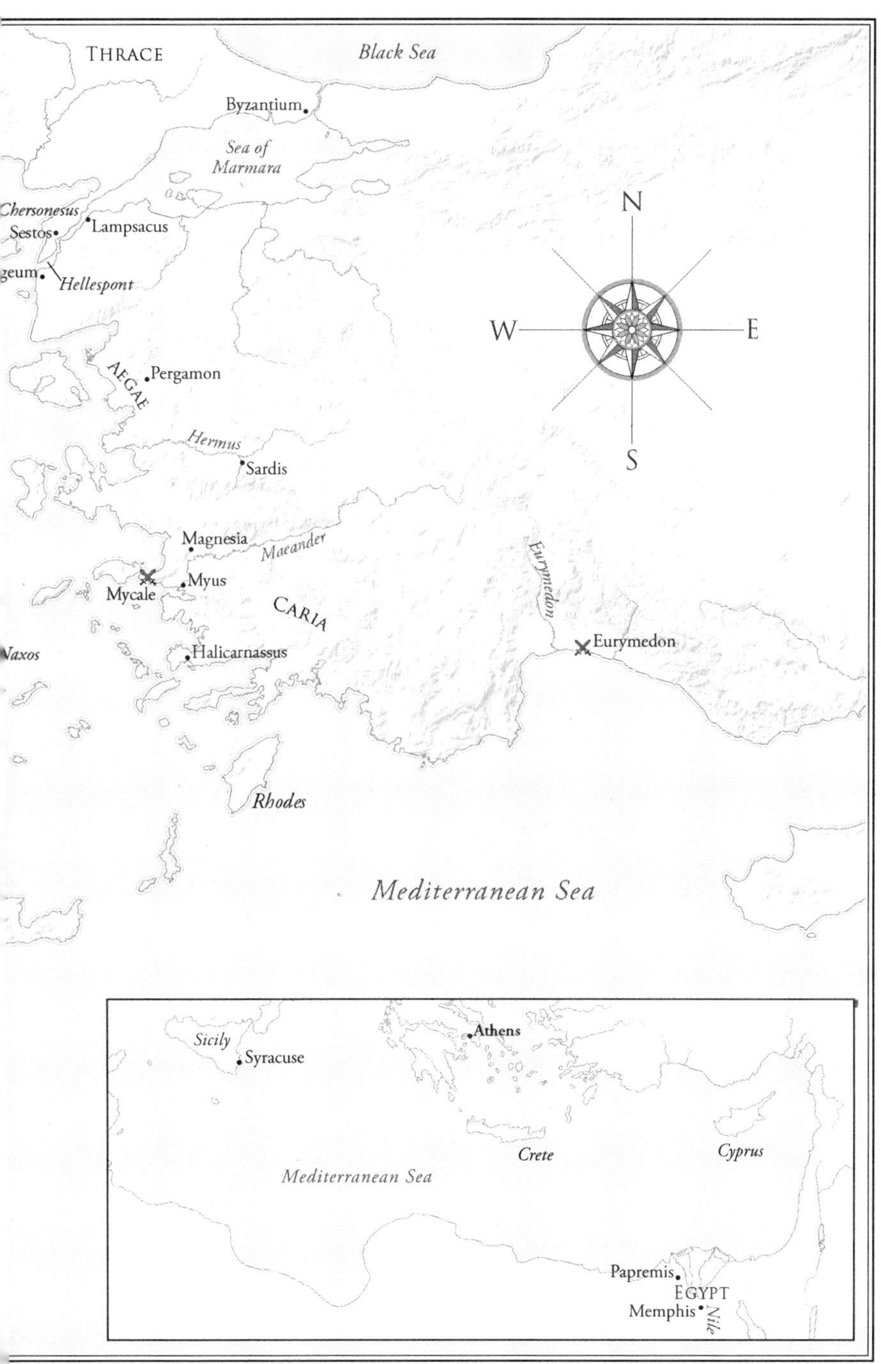
THRACE
Black Sea
Byzantium
Sea of
Marmara
Chersonesus
Sestos
Lampsacus
Hellespont
AEGAE
Pergamon
Hermus
Sardis
Magnesia
Maeander
Myus
Mycale
CARIA
Halicarnassus
Naxos
Eurymedon
Eurymedon
Rhodes
N
W
E
S
Mediterranean Sea
Sicily
Syracuse
Athens
Crete
Cyprus
Mediterranean Sea
Papremis
EGYPT
Memphis
Nile

Themistocles

The Rise and Fall of Athens's Naval Mastermind

Michael Scott

· ANCIENT LIVES ·

Yale
UNIVERSITY PRESS
NEW HAVEN & LONDON

Published with assistance from the foundation established in memory of Amasa Stone Mather of the Class of 1907, Yale College.

Frontispiece: Beehive Mapping.

Yale University Press books may be purchased in quantity for educational, business, or promotional use. For information, please e-mail sales.press@yale.edu (U.S. office) or sales@yaleup.co.uk (U.K. office).

Set in the eYale typeface designed by Matthew Carter, and Louize, designed by Matthieu Cortat, by IDS Infotech Ltd.
Printed in the United States of America.

Library of Congress Control Number: 2025937436
ISBN 978-0-300-25659-8 (hardcover)

A catalogue record for this book is available from the British Library.

Authorized Representative in the EU: Easy Access System Europe, Mustamäe tee 50, 10621 Tallinn, Estonia, gpsr.requests@easproject.com.

10 9 8 7 6 5 4 3 2 1

· ANCIENT LIVES ·

Ancient Lives unfolds the stories of thinkers, writers, kings, queens, conquerors, and politicians from all parts of the ancient world. Readers will come to know these figures in fully human dimensions, complete with foibles and flaws, and will see that the issues they faced – political conflicts, constraints based in gender or race, tensions between the private and public self – have changed very little over the course of millennia.

James Romm
Series Editor

Contents

Note on Dates

Dates that have two numbers separated by a virgule represent the "archon year" (which ran across two calendar years) and are used when events are thought to have happened at some point in that archon year (or across the whole archon year) as opposed to within a calendar year. Dates separated by a dash indicate spans in calendar years.

Themistocles

Prologue

At dawn the earthquake struck. It was taken as a sign – something momentous was about to happen. Looking purely at the numbers, most observers would have agreed that the something momentous would be the obliteration of the Greek fleet – and with it Greek hopes of freedom. The King of Kings, Xerxes, the ruler of the mighty Persian Empire, had personally taken up position on the hilltops above the Straits of Salamis off the coast of Athens, watching his commanders bring their Persian ships together so they could finally teach the Greeks – and particularly the Athenians – a lesson about what happened to those who attempted to defy Persia. He had personally sworn to his supreme god Ahura Mazda that he would do this, marching one of the largest armies and sailing one of the largest fleets ever seen around the Aegean and down across mainland Greece in order to have his day of vengeance.

The date was September 24, 480 BCE. Throughout that day, more and more Persian ships piled up in the wide Saronic Gulf outside the Straits of Salamis, where the Athenian fleet lay in hiding. As night fell, the darkness obscured any sight of the armada massing against the Greeks, saving them from having to look across the waves into the face of oblivion. The outline of the many hulking Persian warships was replaced by an array of burning torches and campfires on the hillsides behind, turning the mighty war machine of Persia into a mirror of the deceptively attractive, star-filled night sky. But nothing could shield the Greeks from the noise, which continued to sweep across the sea throughout the night, of the thousands of Persian sailors and soldiers making their preparations to inflict destruction on their enemy with the rising of the sun.

It is no surprise that in the chilling depth of the night, the courage of the Greek generals in charge of the fleet failed. Calling an emergency council of war, they voted to flee as best they could during the night to escape the Persian monster.

One of the generals, however, believed passionately that they should stand and fight at Salamis. This was a man called Themistocles: an Athenian in his mid-forties, with significant experience not just of the rough-and-tumble of Athenian politics over the previous two decades but also of the other Greek commanders' tendency to get cold feet and decide to turn tail. But that night he realized that this time no amount of winged words, master plans, or even threats, such as he had repeatedly used in the previous weeks and months – successfully – to keep the Greek forces together, would overcome the fear that emanated from every pore of the commanders' skin. There was only one thing to do to ensure that the Greeks stood and fought: give them no other choice. And the only way to do that was to prevent the Greeks from being able to flee. How? Encourage the Persians to tighten their stranglehold on the Straits of Salamis so the Greeks could not get away even if they tried to.

Themistocles seems to have been so sure that this was the right course of action that he ordered a trusted slave, who was himself Persian in origin, to take a small rowboat through the dead of night to the Persian fleet in order to deliver a message directly to the King of Kings himself. Themistocles, the message was to reveal, wanted to defect to the Persians, and as a token of his allegiance, he was prepared to tell the King that the Greeks were intending to flee that night – but if the King sent his fleet immediately to block off the Straits of Salamis, he could prevent their escape and trap them once and for all.

Themistocles thus portrayed himself as a traitor to the Greeks in order to encourage the Persians to encircle them and prevent them from escaping; this, in turn, was intended to ensure that the Greeks stood and fought the Persians at Salamis. Themistocles was taking a huge risk. He had no way of knowing whether his slave would make it through to the Persian fleet, or then reach the Persian King, or indeed whether his message would be believed and be acted upon, and thus achieve his goal of forcing the Greeks to fight. But he did know that if his messenger were discovered by the Greeks en route to the Persians, they would interpret his actions as treasonous and turn on him in short order. He was thus risking his life to ensure that the long-awaited battle between the Persians and the Greeks was fought the next day.

As the night waned, news started to trickle in that the Persian fleet had tightened its stranglehold on the straits. By the time dawn broke on September 25, the Greek commanders – including Themistocles – saw that they were trapped. There was nothing to do but fight. Themistocles had the battle he had worked so hard to bring about.

And against all the odds the Greeks emerged from that conflict victorious. The ancient historian and moralist Plutarch, writing in the late first century CE and echoing an earlier Greek poet, Simonides, claimed their victory to be the most brilliant exploit ever performed at sea by either Greeks or "barbarians." Plutarch attributed the victory to the courage and enthusiasm of all who fought in the battle, but particularly to the good judgment and cleverness of Themistocles. The "trick" he played on the Persian King, thanks to the successful outcome of the battle for the Greeks, had come to be remembered, on balance, as a magnificent piece of manipulation by the heroic Athenian rather than the act of a traitor keen to ensure his own survival if the Persians prevailed.[1]

Other commentators offered even greater praise. Writing during the Peloponnesian War in the second half of the fifth century BCE, just half a century after Themistocles' actions at Salamis, the Greek historian Thucydides claimed that the Athenian Themistocles, along with another Greek general, the Spartan Pausanias, were the "most illustrious Greeks of their time."[2]

"Most illustrious" seems an odd epithet for a man whose high-point was the calculated encouragement of the enemy to encircle his own forces in order to ensure they were left with no option but to fight for their survival. And even granting that this risky move produced a great Greek victory, the wider story of Themistocles' (and the Spartan Pausanias's) life reveals a regular pattern of bold (and successful) moves matched by an equal number of failures, ending for both of them with a fall from grace and permanent exile from Greece. Is this the story we might expect of the most illustrious Greeks of the early fifth century BCE, the dawn of Greece's so-called Golden Age?

Crucially, Themistocles merited this title, according to Thucydides, because he seemingly achieved his success on the basis of his "natural powers": his natural wit, intellect, perception, and judgment. Through these natural gifts, alongside his "speed of reaction," he was "without equal at improvising the right course of action."[3] Thucydides received much praise for his writings and for his judgment of character, including that of Themistocles. Yet in some ways, Thucydides' attribution of Themistocles' brilliance to his "natural powers" makes Themistocles a rather one-dimensional character: a man who was simply naturally good at working out what to do. That vision of Themistocles is often said to be confirmed by the famous Ostia portrait bust of him, which underlines his physical strength, portrayed in his square—almost bullish—face, the decisiveness and determination of his set jaw, the deep-set eyes and firm mouth (figure 1). Although the bust itself dates from a period much later than Themistocles' own lifetime, scholars and others argue that it replicates images of him created during his lifetime or just after: "a copy of a contemporary likeness," indeed perhaps "the first true portrait of an individual European that we have."[4]

Yet this image—both literary and artistic—of one of the most illustrious Greeks of his time, as a man blessed with decisiveness and intuition, is far from complete. First and foremost it overlooks the fact, highlighted already, that along with the several risky but ultimately successful and vindicated calls Themistocles made, such as the one at Salamis, were many that did not turn out so successfully; furthermore, later in life he *was* exiled from Greece as a traitor. This view of him also misses the crucial point that Themistocles' story is not one of nature alone but also of the crucial impact of nurture: contributing not only to the development of his skills but also of his worldview, his ambitions, his methods, and ultimately of the decisions that defined his life and reputation. And finally, accepting at face value the literary and artistic image of a man destined for success undercuts the crucial part that writers of history and biography have had to play in the decades and centuries after his death in spotlighting particular moments of Themistocles' career as defining elements of his character and reputation, thus shaping his "illustrious" legacy.

Marble portrait of Themistocles from Ostia (Ostia Museum. Photo by Sailko, CC BY 3.0, https://creativecommons.org/licenses/by/3.0/deed.en)

It is thus my hope in this biography to offer a more human story of Themistocles, a man not born for success, who was, in equal measure to his moments of decisive (and successful) action, at times uncertain, unprepared, and unsuccessful, and who did not always know the right course to take – but who at various points during his lifetime and, most important, after his death, was recognized as having been crucial to Greece's story and its success. My aim is to create a more useful and thought-provoking portrait of the man who came to be recognized as the most illustrious Greek of his time – one that will enrich our understanding of Themistocles, of the ancient Mediterranean world, and, ultimately, of how real lives are led, things achieved, and reputations won.

CHAPTER ONE

Ambiguous Beginnings

The deme – the smallest unit of Athenian civic organization, akin to a local borough in the United Kingdom (and in some U.S. cities) today – of Phrearrhioi sat in the lower half of the territory of Attica, which stretches out into the Aegean like a stubby finger on the body of mainland Greece. Roughly eighteen miles from the city of Athens itself, the deme of Phrearrhioi was a sleepy backwater on the border zone of the coastal and agricultural heartland communities of this area of Attica. In 524/3 BCE, a son was born to a man called Neocles, who was a member of the deme of Phrearrhioi.[1] The son's name was Themistocles.

Neocles was no Athenian aristocrat, yet he does not seem to have been poor either. He was, according to Plutarch, "not one of the particularly distinguished men at Athens," but according to the first-century BCE biographer Cornelius Nepos, he was "of a good family."[2] His upper-middle-class social position thus mirrors something of the geographical position of his deme: on the border between the coastal area (traditionally associated with the increasingly powerful trading class of Attica at the time) and the agricultural plains of inland Attica (traditionally associated with the older elite ruling families).

Themistocles' mother, on the other hand, is more controversial. The late-second-century CE writer Athenaeus relates that Themistocles' mother was Abrotonon, a prostitute, who came not from Attica but from Thrace, to the north. Other ancient writers suggest she came from Asia Minor.[3] Despite these disagreements, crucially, all the ancient sources portray Themistocles' mother as a non-Athenian, from the edges of the Greek world. In the ancient Athens of 524/3 BCE, this put Themistocles within a liminal category of citizenship on the edge of society. He was what was termed in ancient Greek a *nothos*—a child of a citizen father and a non-citizen mother—with one foot in Athenian society and one foot outside it.

Themistocles was by no means alone in this position. Just three years earlier, in 527, the ruler of Athens, Peisistratus, a tyrant (*turannos*) who had seized power in 546/5, had died. Peisistratus himself had had a son, Hegesistratus, with a woman from Argos, a long-established and well-respected Greek city-state in the Peloponnese. But even so Hegesistratus was a nothos and was not one of the sons to whom Peisistratus's power passed on his death (it passed instead to his fully Athenian son Hippias). If a man could be passed over in late-sixth-century Athens because his mother came from another powerful mainland Greek city, imagine the reaction to a mother coming from a non-Greek family at the very boundaries of the civilized Greek world.[4]

It may be that Themistocles' position was a little more assured than this. Some commentators have argued that Neocles lived in the area of the Chersonesus (the modern-day Gallipoli peninsula) in Chalcidian Thrace, at this time still dominated by a string of Athenian colonies.[5] Themistocles' mother may then have been from another Athenian colony in the region – "Thracian" but sort of Athenian-Thracian. Neocles, it has been argued, went out as an early settler under the command of a member of an elite Athenian family soon after Peisistratus had taken firm possession of the position of turannos. Neocles' return to Athens was similarly motivated by the return of Miltiades, of the same elite family, to take up the archonship (position of chief magistrate) in Athens in 524/3, the year Themistocles was born. Thus, Themistocles' father, while of no particular distinction, may have been closer to the center of political activity at Athens than might first have been assumed, thanks to his connection to Miltiades, and his mother may have been more Athenian than the later sources make out.

It is possible, then, that Themistocles was born in Thrace, or perhaps in central Athens, or perhaps in the sleepy deme of Phrearrhioi, where his father acquired property and was inscribed on the deme citizenship lists. His parents may have been a simple upper-middle-class citizen father and a foreign (perhaps prostitute) mother, or a well-connected father and a mother from a far-flung Athenian colony newly arrived back in Athens. Themistocles' own position may thus have been one of slight "otherness" (if he was the product of "colonial" Athenians) or more outright "otherness" (if his mother came from farther afield and a more salubrious background). But one thing is clear – he was far from being a member of the one of the elite aristocratic families of Athens. Indeed Themistocles' name literally translates as "new fame" (meaning new to fame, newly famous), perhaps reinforcing the sense of his origins as not being those of the traditional elite aristocracy.

The surviving inscriptional evidence from ancient Athens has demonstrated beyond doubt that even though Peisistratus, of the elite Peisistratid family, was the ruler of Athens up to his death in

527, after which his son Hippias took up the title of turannos, there was still room for other elite families to occupy important official positions in Athens like that of archon. In 525/4, the year before Themistocles was born, for example, we know that the "eponymous" archon, the chief magistrate of the polis of Athens, was a man called Cleisthenes, son of Megacles, of the Alcmaeonid family – one of the other elite, distinguished, and historic families in Athens. In 524/3, as we have seen, the archon was Miltiades, part of the Philaid aristocratic family. But in 522/1, the archon was the grandson of Peisistratus (also called Peisistratus) of the Peisistratid family.

While the archonship was thus the prize in a game of musical chairs among the elite families of Athens during Themistocles' youngest years, up to the age of six or seven, he would have grown up in his *oikos* (home), most likely within the deme of Phrearrhioi. He would have had a *paidagogos* – an educated slave who acted as an early instructor. This paidagogos would have been one of a number of slaves owned by Themistocles' family, for Athens was, like all Greece, a slave-owning society, and current estimates suggest that each modestly well-off household had on average three or four slaves.

Once he reached age six or seven, Themistocles would have attended a school, with his paidagogos accompanying him to and from the building and keeping an eye on him during lessons. We should not, however, imagine a large school with hundreds of children following a state-authorized curriculum – Athens had no such thing. Instead schools were all privately run by individuals who taught their own preferred courses. They also all tended to be small – so small that children did not speak of "going to school," but rather of "going to the home of their teacher." Themistocles may thus have been in a class of ten or fewer students.

While there was no set curriculum, we know that the general shape of his education would have focused around ensuring he could read and write, and had a good knowledge of literature and some basic math, as well as placing a strong emphasis on music and sport. Indeed, we are told that Hipparchus, another of Peisistratus's fully Athenian sons, who held great influence in Athens alongside his turannos brother Hippias, was a particular patron of the arts, music, and literature and saw them as essential for the education of Athenians. According to the fourth-century BCE philosopher Plato, it was Hipparchus who first brought Homer's *Iliad* and *Odyssey* to Athens, requiring them to be recited in full at the Athenian Panathenaia festival celebrations, because he wanted to rule over wise people and believed that nobody should be excluded from education. In an effort to educate the people not just of the city but of the Attic countryside as well, Hipparchus was even said to have ordered the inscribing of important phrases and ideas on herm statues (representations of the god Hermes) at crossroads across Attica.[6]

When he was around seven to ten years old, it is unlikely that Themistocles was aware of Hipparchus's push for the arts. But his schooling may well have been affected by it. Plato had one of the protagonists in his writings comment that boys learned long passages of literature by heart so that the examples might inspire and be imitated by them. Central to their learning were the *Iliad* and *Odyssey* because, according to Plato, in Homer boys saw how men should behave. Equally, instruction in music—how to play particular instruments and how to recite to music—was considered, at least in the fifth and fourth centuries BCE, to be an essential ingredient of a good education. As Plato put it with regard to the benefits of learning about music, "In this way they become more gentle, more efficient in their speech and action—for the whole of man's life requires rhythm and harmony."[7]

Plutarch comments that as a pupil at school, Themistocles was intelligent and full of energy. As will be instantly recognized by any teacher today, this is a coded way of saying in a school report that the child was not the best behaved one in the class. According to Plutarch, Themistocles was also not particularly interested in subjects which were "character-forming," or "aimed at pleasant or liberal accomplishment." It thus seems that Themistocles did not care much for the instruction in music he may have received, intended to make him more cultured, controlled, and better balanced. Indeed, Plutarch also recounts that in later life Themistocles was mocked for his lack of musical know-how in not knowing how to tune a lyre or play a harp.[8]

Instead, Plutarch notes, as a young boy Themistocles was interested in developing his intelligence, gaining practical knowledge, and sharpening his skills in rhetoric – even spending his break times composing speeches to defend or prosecute one or other of his fellow pupils for some playground antic. In the fourth century CE, some 850 years after Themistocles was a schoolboy, a teacher of rhetoric and wisdom in the eastern Roman Empire, Libanius of Antioch, wrote a series of mock court declamations based around particular moments in history as learning tools for his pupils. Two of these focus on Themistocles' early life – one written from the perspective of his father and one from Themistocles' own. In imitating Neocles, Libanius argues that he sent Themistocles to school because he knew education was important for the soul. But, Libanius has Neocles argue, from the outset Themistocles did not listen to his paidagogos or teachers, even when they punished him.[9] That Libanius, 850 years later, would base some of his imaginative law-court speeches around the issue of Themistocles' education underlines how important a figure in history Themistocles had become. And while we cannot accept at face value any of the details, it is striking that all the ancient commentators seem to have been keen to make it clear that Themistocles was a handful in his early years.

In many ways, this later characterization of Themistocles – as a child pushing back at the authorities around him and spending his time focusing on trying to persuade his fellow pupils through the power of words to follow some course of action – reflects the moments in his later life for which Themistocles would ultimately become famous and be remembered – as someone advocating, scheming, and manipulating people into pursuing an unpopular but ultimately successful course of action, as at Salamis. But that image of an upstart, of someone rebelling and throwing his opinion around, also mirrors the wider state of Athenian politics at the time of Themistocles' birth and during his youth.

When Peisistratus died in 527 BCE, we need to imagine an Athens – and its wider territory of Attica – in a state of evolution and imbalance. On one hand, the city was under a tyranny, but not one that excluded all other voices from having their say, as the shifting position of archon among a number of Athens's elite families makes clear. The population of Attica also had new symbols, places, and moments of community celebration and recognition to gather around, owing to the efforts of Peisistratus. It was during his time as turannos that Athens, for example, began the celebration of the Great Dionysia – its pan-Athenian festival of worship for the god Dionysus that included the tradition of putting on, over several days, tragedies, satyr plays, and comedies; it was at the Great Dionysia that the works of Aeschylus, Sophocles, and Euripides were first performed. Peisistratus is also credited with elaborating the pan-Athenian festival in honor of Demeter and Persephone at Eleusis, and with enlarging Athens's role within the wider Greek world in the celebrations of Apollo on the island of Delos.

But Attica was also a community in the grip of a slow but sure societal evolution, which had been ongoing for over a century, and which was increasingly spotlighting the imbalance in political and economic power among its different classes and communities – particularly its old aristocratic elites, its newer wealthy trading class, and the wider mass of the population. We are told in the ancient sources that this continual evolution and shifting political and economic power balance had created a number of different viewpoints on how society should be run and how much say each group should have in the process of government. Such differences of opinion often overlapped with geographical location. Those who lived "on the plains" in the traditional agricultural and farming areas of inland Attica, generally favored an older, oligarchic vision for the future, led by the old elite aristocratic families who controlled the land they lived on. Those who lived "on the coast," often involved with the newly burgeoning trading networks and benefiting from the access to wealth these brought, sought a "mixed/balanced/middle of the road constitution," while those, variously identified as living "in [or beyond] the hills" – presumably the poor mainstream of the Athenian population – hankered after a political system in which everyone had a full say.[10]

Themistocles, as we have seen, was born to a family that came from a deme on the borders of a coastal and inland plains region, on the borders of these two groups and to some extent, depending on who Themistocles' mother was, on the borderline of Athenian society itself. Themistocles was born into, and grew up, during a period of social, cultural, political, and economic evolution and unrest which was soon to burst into revolution. As a headstrong boy who railed against the authority of his schoolmasters and sought to convince others of his views, Themistocles thus comes across as nothing less than a mirror of the changing world in which he was born.

CHAPTER TWO

A World in Crisis

The day was supposed to be joyful, a religious celebration of the favor Athens received from its patron goddess Athena, and a mass demonstration of the honor and reverence in which the Athenians held their patron. Thousands of Athenian citizens processed through the city to bring her sacred statue on the Acropolis offerings as tokens of their love and respect. Thousands more gathered to watch the procession, meet and rejoice with one another, eat, drink, and celebrate the fortune of their city. What there was not supposed to be was murder.

In 514 BCE, when Themistocles was around ten years old, fully immersed in his schooling (or not, as the case may have been), his world changed, owing to unprecedented events unfolding at the Panathenaia. The first he would have heard of them, most likely, would have been through reports making their way back to his home deme of Phrearrhioi from those who had attended the festival.

As the procession assembled to deliver the ritual gifts to the sacred statue of Athena on the Acropolis, two men, Harmodius and Aristogeiton, had come forward, taking out daggers hidden on their persons, and attacked the turannos Hippias. Hippias managed to escape, but his brother Hipparchus, who had taken such delight in the cultural education of his fellow Athenians, was killed in the melee. As the news started filtering back to Phrearrhioi of Hipparchus's murder, it was followed by news of yet more killing. Hippias's bodyguard had not only managed to defend Hippias but had in turn killed one of the assailants: Harmodius. Aristogeiton, despite initially escaping, was soon captured. According to some ancient sources, he was tortured for information. According to others, Hippias himself killed him in rage at his brother's murder.

The ten-year-old Themistocles may not have understood exactly what had passed. Indeed, few perhaps realized at the time how much this incident would upend the delicate tap dance of power that had existed in Athens between the elite aristocratic families and the wider power blocs of Athenian society, over the previous thirty years. But all the sources agree that the main outcome of these murders was that Hippias tipped from "wise fellow and natural-born statesman" into a cruel, embittered, and fearful tyrant who ordered the execution of anyone he suspected of plotting against him. Rival aristocratic families, who had once shared the different positions of power within the city (such as the Alcmaeonids), now seem to have chosen – or been pushed – to leave Athens and go into exile. Some of the ancient sources suggest that Hippias took to murdering those he felt posed a threat.[1] For more than three years, Athens seems to have been frozen in the grip of a real tyrant.

We presume that Themistocles' education continued during this tense period from 514 on – indeed, it would probably have expanded. Neocles, or Themistocles' paidagogos, would probably have started taking Themistocles, starting at about age twelve, to the *palaistra,* the wrestling school. Here the final element of his education would have been instilled in him: the ability to compete, and preferably win, against his fellow pupils in numerous contact sports like boxing, wrestling and the pankration (the "all-power" event in which there were almost no rules and the only goal was to force one's opponent into submission). Each day the students would have prepared themselves to face one another and test their skills in full view of their fellow students and teachers. The smell of the sweat caused by the heat of the day, the exertion, and the nerves of the young students would have mixed with the cries of pain, anguish, and victory that echoed around the wall of the palaistra as these young boys were taught time and again that competition with one another was the route to improvement, skill, victory, honor, and fame.

As Themistocles continued his educational journey, we hear nothing in the ancient sources of his family being directly affected by Hippias's turn toward full tyranny. Perhaps he was to some extent protected by his father's social status outside the circle of elite families that posed a threat to Hippias, or by his family's geographical location in the countryside rather than in the city of Athens itself; and even perhaps by his own status as a nothos, which made him largely irrelevant to the power politics of the day. But we can be fairly sure that Hippias's actions would have been a regular topic of conversation in the household. We should imagine Themistocles, as he started the next phase of his journey toward adulthood, listening to his father's concerns and worries expressed privately at home as to what might potentially befall them, catching snippets of worried conversations in the street, asking his paidagogos to help him understand why people were behaving more cautiously and carefully than before and to explain what was generating this atmosphere of increasing fear.

In 510, Themistocles turned fourteen. He was in Athenian eyes still a boy, four years away from the ceremony in which he would be formally accepted into his deme as an adult. And while we know nothing for certain of Themistocles' movements over this period, it is unlikely that he was not directly affected by the latest events. For in 511, a Spartan army had landed at Phaleron, on the coast of Attica (one of the ports of the ancient city), with the express intention of ridding Athens of its tyrant. Herodotus, the Greek historian who, in the 420s BCE, wrote a history of events leading up to the Greco-Persian Wars, explained that Sparta took such an interest in internal Athenian politics at this time only because of the Alcmaeonid family, who had taken themselves into exile after the murder of Hipparchus. For after having tried themselves, along with their fellow Athenian exiles, to take on Hippias without success, the Alcmaeonids had sought to harness the support of the *omphalos,* the navel of the earth, the oracular sanctuary of Apollo at Delphi.[2]

Oracular consultation was at the heart of how the ancient Greeks understood the will of their gods. Given that they believed the gods were in control of everything, it made sense for them to want to find out whether those gods were in favor of a particular course of action, because if they were not, it was simply not worth doing. Consulting the gods in advance of undertaking an endeavor, or consulting them on how best to achieve a particular desired outcome, was a regular feature of Greek activity. It could be done in a myriad of ways, each requiring a different amount of time, effort, and financial input, from consulting the cheaper oracle-peddlers on the streets to hiring a more official interpreter of signs (who might read the "signs" in a flight of birds or the entrails of an animal to divine the view of the gods) to investing the time, effort, and money in traveling to a sanctuary where the suppliant could put a question to a particular god, normally via a priestly intermediary. Of all the sanctuaries Greeks could travel to, none was more famous than the oracular sanctuary of Apollo at Delphi, where the Pythian priestess would receive the question and deliver a response thought to be directly from Apollo himself. Responses from the oracle, given the prestige of the sanctuary and the direct nature of the engagement with the god, were seen as having huge value, significance, and weight attached to them. They were, in many ways, the gold standard in divine indications of what suppliants should do.

The sanctuary at Delphi at the time that the Alcmaeonids sought to harness the support of the oracle was in the middle of a massive building project: the temple had been destroyed by fire in the middle of the century and since that time the sanctuary authorities had spent decades raising the funds not only to rebuild but to expand. The Alcmaeonids, having fled in exile from Athens to take up residence at Delphi, were said to have taken on the contract to oversee the completion of the front of the new temple of Apollo and at their own expense to have finished it in Parian marble rather than the limestone originally planned. Delphi was in their debt, and it was at this time that, whenever the Spartans came to consult the oracle about any matter, the oracle told them that they must first free the Athenians from tyranny. The Spartans understandably felt they were being directed by the gods to intervene in Athens's internal civic strife.

Themistocles and his family were not in the direct path of the Spartan invading force, which landed at the port of Phaleron and headed north directly to Athens, but they were not a long way from it. They would no doubt have heard quickly about the attack, have retreated from their daily businesses to their homes, and waited to see what happened next. They would probably soon have started receiving firsthand accounts of the conflict from those who had been near at hand or perhaps even involved: how Sparta's first attempt to unseat Hippias had not succeeded because Hippias had called in his own favors with the Thessalians to the north, whose ruler came with a thousand horsemen thundering to Hippias's aid. They would have heard how the Spartan general leading the attack had been killed and his remaining troops forced back into their ships at Phaleron.

But there would have been no swift return to normalcy, as everyone waited to see what the Spartans would do next. They soon returned, headed this time by their own king, Cleomenes. He approached by land up from the Peloponnese, across the Isthmus, and then into the northern half of Attica, meeting the Thessalian cavalry in open battle. This time the Spartans stood firm against the terrifying sight of a seemingly impervious line of huge, muscle-bound Thessalian horses thundering toward them, and they managed to break up the cavalry line, picking the riders off to leave dead men and horses strewn across the battlefield, while the remainder fled back to their homeland.

This clash took place farther from Phrearrhioi than the previous battle, so perhaps news of events took longer to filter through to it, leaving Themistocles and his family, as well as friends and neighbors, uncertain of what had happened and of what might happen next. As the Spartans approached the city of Athens, accompanied by the Athenian families who had retreated into exile, Hippias and his remaining supporters were forced to take refuge on the Acropolis, in the heart of the city. This huge, prominent natural rock fortress became the center of a stalemate. Hippias and his supporters looked down on an impregnable ring of Spartans and Athenians surrounding them, the noise of their encampment, the clang of their weapons, and the braying of their horses echoing up the rock face to the top of the Acropolis, reminding them night and day that they were trapped. Long might they have remained so, if it had not been for a plot to smuggle Hippias's sons away to safety; it was discovered and his sons were captured. With this leverage, the Spartans forced Hippias to give up his liberty in return for his sons' lives. He abandoned the Acropolis and was exiled from Athens, coming finally to rest at Sigeum in the Hellespont, in the northeastern Aegean.

Themistocles was fourteen as these rival Greek communities trampled over Attica, fighting both for and against its tyrant ruler, and as that ruler was besieged on the Acropolis, the religious and symbolic heart of the city. With Hippias gone, the Spartans and Thessalians departed. From Phrearrhioi, as a boy who did not yet have a recognized adult voice in the system, Themistocles must have felt powerless to affect what might happen to him, his family, and his way of life.

The political vacuum left in Athens was once again filled with competing aristocratic voices, from some of the same families that had been working behind the scenes to orchestrate change. Cleisthenes, an Alcmaeonid, who had been archon in 525/4 during the power-sharing era of Hippias's tyranny just before Themistocles was born, and subsequently driven into exile after Hipparchus's death in 514, had been central to the Alcmaeonid efforts to persuade the Spartans (via the Delphic oracle) to free Athens from Hippias, and he now once again came to the fore in Athenian politics. He was no young radical but an experienced political operator in his sixties. Yet his voice was by no means alone. His great rival in this period was another aristocratic Athenian, Isagoras, who had remained in Athens throughout Hippias's tyranny and who wanted as little to change as possible after Hippias's removal. For almost two years, there was no certainty as to which way the wind would blow. Themistocles continued his studies, not knowing to what extent his world would change, his teenage years once again defined by uncertainty and a sense of powerlessness. And then, in 508/7, as he turned sixteen, Cleisthenes, in an appeal directly to the citizens of Athens, "added the *demos* – the mass of the people – to his faction" by suggesting a complete reappraisal of the Athenian political system.[3]

So just as Themistocles was about to come of age, the political system of Athens was turned on its head. The 140 demes of Attica were organized into 30 groupings called *trittyes*. Each *trittys* (thirding) was formed of one village (a deme) or group of villages drawn from one of three different kinds of region: coastal, inland/countryside, or urban. Three trittyes – one coastal, one rural, and one urban – were then combined to form an artificial "tribe." These new ten tribes of Athens – whereas previously there had been only four, ostensibly "kinship" tribes – were given new names, which Cleisthenes saw to it received the approval of the god Apollo through the oracle at Delphi.[4]

Themistocles' deme of Phrearrhioi was in a coastal trittys and was twinned with the urban trittys of Scambonidae, which occupied the northern part of the city of Athens, and a countryside trittys (name unknown), to form the new tribe of Leontis. The tribe was named after the hero Leos, a son of Orpheus, who had sacrificed his three daughters in order to save his city from famine. Themistocles' home political unit, of which he was just now old enough to become a part, was thus united with other distant parts of Attica. His fellow tribesmen in these other trittyes were people he had never met or with whom perhaps he did not have much in common. And that was the point. Cleisthenes' tribal reforms sought to cut through the regional- and family-based traditional alliances, in particular those between aristocratic families, giving the people instead a new unit, the deme-based tribe, through which to take part in the politics of Athens. A fresh start. But with every fresh start comes even more uncertainty, upheaval, confusion, and worry, something that no doubt Themistocles was encountering and feeling on a daily basis.

Confusion also arose because neither Themistocles nor anyone else in Athens was sure that this new system would be brought into force. However much Cleisthenes had added the demos to his faction, he could not force Athens – and particularly his aristocratic rivals – to adopt his proposals. Isagoras, who held the position of archon in 508/7, technically with the power to block any attempt at constitutional change, was obviously opposed to the changes. Yet he went one step farther and called once again for external help. The Spartan king Cleomenes, who had freed Athens of Hippias and was a supporter of Isagoras (and allegedly had designs on his wife), now demanded the expulsion of Cleisthenes and the abandonment of his plans for reform. When Athens seemingly balked at the Spartans' request – principally because no city-state likes being told what to do by another – Cleomenes returned with his forces to Attic soil. Cleisthenes and his Alcmaeonids withdrew into exile once again, and Isagoras, who had seen at first hand the entirety of the tyranny of Hippias, now seems to have attempted something similar. With Spartan support, Isagoras exiled another seven hundred Athenian families, attempted to disband the governing council, the Boule, of the city and put himself in charge, along with three hundred of his closest associates.

What would Themistocles, age sixteen or seventeen, have made of this from the perspective of his home in Phrearrhioi? In the previous few years, Athens had been invaded three times by the Spartans; seen a tyrant go to extreme lengths to hang on to power and then be forced out; suffered uncertainty and confusion as rival factions grappled to reshape Athens's political system; and had its civic system completely uprooted and overhauled, its political apparatus suspended, and power returned to a new closed-rank elite. No doubt Themistocles would have been confused and uncertain. But it is likely that he would also have been angry: angry that others were repeatedly deciding his life for him, not just as a growing teenager, but as an emerging citizen of Athens.

That anger was felt by many more than just Themistocles. In fact, the sources reflect that this latest round of changes abandoning the traditional political organs of Athenian society was more than the Athenians would collectively stand. Herodotus tells us that the people of Athens rose up and converged on the city, trapping Isagoras, Cleomenes, and his Spartan troops at the Acropolis, where just two years earlier Cleomenes had trapped Hippias.[5] There they were besieged for three days by the people of Athens – a huge pulsating crowd united by fear and anger. We have no way of knowing whether Themistocles was one of those people, but it is definitely possible – indeed probable – that he was, as an intelligent and hot-headed sixteen-year-old on the brink of adulthood. Over those three long days, standing, sitting, camping at the base of the Acropolis, probably chanting and shouting to unnerve those trapped above them, discussing with their new citizen comrades at arms options for storming the Acropolis, eagerly seeking any sign that that the besieged were either trying to escape or willing to submit, Themistocles may well have felt that finally he was doing something to direct events rather than be directed by them.

After three days of this threatening tumult, Isagoras and Cleomenes capitulated and agreed to withdraw from Athens. They left humiliated, while those who had surrounded them on the Acropolis drifted back, drunk with the sweet elixir of victory, to their homes. The exiled families, including that of Cleisthenes, were recalled. In the face of this second attempt at harsh tyrannical rule and its quashing by the mass of the people, it is no surprise that now Cleisthenes' reforms found formal favor. The deme became the basis for all civic engagement, rights, and responsibilities. And the demes – through their new trittyes, which grouped them into new tribes – were the pathways through which every deme member got to take part in the political system of Athens. This was *isonomia* – equality before the law for all. Themistocles' deme was now resolutely connected with new demes spread across Attica, and with that reorganization came new possibilities for how people, from a wider group than the traditional elite aristocratic families, could gain renown, favor, and power.

At the same time, there was an even more important (at least for Themistocles) change to the Athenian political system instigated by Cleisthenes. All free men living in the demes created by Cleisthenes' new political system were made eligible to be citizens of Athens. Themistocles' ambiguous status, owing to his parentage, was now resolved and the path was clear for him, as he turned eighteen, to become a fully fledged citizen of Athens within its new system of isonomia.

It was a heady time for anyone to come of age, but particularly for one like Themistocles: coming from an ambiguous social status, intelligent, eager, keen to convince others of his views, and not very responsive to rules. Athens had fundamentally changed in order to break the chains of old aristocratic alliances and influence and to encourage more voices and more participation within its society. Yet it was also a period of continued uncertainty and fear. In fact, the Athenians were so fearful for their security immediately after the expulsion of Sparta and the adoption of Cleisthenes' reforms that they even reached out to the Persian Great King, Darius I, across the Aegean for support in ensuring the city's survival!

The Athenians were right to be concerned. In 506, Cleomenes mustered another army of Spartans and other cities from the

Peloponnese, and made plans for these groups, along with the Boeotians and the Chalcidians, whose territory lay to the north and east of Athens, to make simultaneous attacks on Attica. Cleomenes' plan was to reinstall Isagoras as leader in Athens. Attica found itself caught "in a ring of foes," surrounded by enemies.[6] Its citizen hoplite (infantry) army – now composed of one hoplite regiment from each of its new tribes – set out to meet Cleomenes on the western boundary of Attica at Eleusis.

The name "hoplites" comes from their *hoplon* – the round shield three feet wide which each solder carried. In addition to this each hoplite wore a metal helmet, breastplate, and greaves, and carried a spear and a short sword. Each soldier had to pay for and provide his own armor, which meant that hoplites were by definition fairly wealthy members of society (they often brought slaves with them to help carry their equipment). So while Athens's army was representative of its new political system in that it had soldiers from each of its new tribes, it was not representative of the full spectrum of Athenian society, but only those sections of above-average wealth.

Yet birth matters little in the heat of battle: metal crashing against metal, the sickening cries as swords pierced and mutilated the body. The confusion for individual soldiers, whose field of vision was narrowed from within their helmet, about the direction from which the next attack might come. The aching tiredness seeping across their bodies as they moved to fight, defend, kill, protect, advance, and survive. The sheer relief and jubilation at the sight of the enemy giving up first.

That relief and jubilation were felt by the band of elite Athenian hoplites, who were victorious and managed to scatter the forces of Cleomenes, after a number of his Peloponnesian allies decided to withdraw from the battle. Drunk with the success of their first victory, the Athenian forces marched on, like wolves stalking their prey, to confront the Boeotians in battle. Having destroyed them, they moved, the same day, to take on the Chalcidians. The Athenian force of blood-hungry soldiers, spurred on by their victories, decimated them.

The Athenians imprisoned as many Boeotians and Chalcidians as they could: these defeated soldiers, exhausted, deflated, wounded, were shackled in heavy chains and led away, later to be ransomed for a hefty fee. At the same time, the Athenians took for themselves much of the land of Euboea, the home of the Chalcidians, and settled their own colonists there. On the Acropolis, in the heart of Athens, they dedicated the chains used to shackle their prisoners and set aside a tenth of the ransom money to dedicate a bronze statue of a chariot and four horses to their patron deity Athena. The chariot stood facing visitors who climbed the staircase to access the summit of the Acropolis and carried an inscription marking the Athenians' great victory. It was the first statement of a new victorious people.[7]

We do not know whether Themistocles fought in the Athenian army that took on the Spartans, Boeotians, and Chalcidians – he would have been seventeen turning eighteen, and eighteen was the usual age at which Athenians were expected to serve. But without doubt he would have lived the story of their fight and their victory. Athens had emerged from a sustained period of uncertainty, fear, and change to be surrounded by its enemies, and then, in quick succession, to triumph over them all. These battles had not simply been a test of Athens's military strength; they had also been a test of its new political system. And the city had passed with flying colors.

Themistocles turned eighteen and had the path cleared for him to become a full Athenian citizen, as the system of isonomia proved its value and offered a vision of what heights it could carry

Athens to (or rather, carry those in Athenian society of above-average wealth who could afford to supply the armor to fight as hoplites on behalf of the system of isonomia). What stood out perhaps most clearly at the time was the way in which Athens, and the Athenians, responded strongly to any attempt by one individual to impose his will on the people, especially when that individual brought in outsiders to support him. They had risen up when Hippias had attempted to impose his will with the help of the Thessalians, and when Isagoras had attempted to do the same with the help of Sparta and later the Boeotians and Chalcidians. An acute observer like the young Themistocles would perhaps have been able to perceive the crucial tipping point in the Athenians' psyche between wanting strong leadership and wanting to preserve their freedom and integrity. Positioning oneself at that tipping point was the key to success in Athens. But could any one individual perform such a precarious balancing act for long?

CHAPTER THREE

Tipping Points

Ships were left burning or sunk. Port buildings destroyed. People dead in the streets.

This was not the glorious future the Athenians had anticipated after their decimation of their Spartan, Boeotian, and Chalcidian adversaries. But those three groups were by no means the only enemies of Athens littered across Greece. The latest attack, on the Athenian port of Phaleron, had come from the island of Aegina, just off the southeastern coast of Attica. The Aeginetans, a formidable sea power in the region and long-term enemy of Athens, had set sail for the coast of Athens and laid waste to its port.

Themistocles was in his early twenties and would soon have heard about this latest attack. He was no longer primarily resident in his sleepy deme in rural Attica, but settled in and about the city of Athens, with a home in the deme of Melite. It was not an elite neighborhood; the place where the bodies of criminals were disposed of was not far from his house.[1] Plutarch would later claim that he liked to exercise at the gymnasium of Cynosarges. This enclosure – both a religious sanctuary and a public gymnasium – sat just outside the city walls on its southern side, on the banks of the Ilissus River. The temple there was dedicated to Heracles and other members of his family, and the whole complex had a long association with nothoi, children of a citizen father and a foreign mother. Heracles himself was claimed as something of a nothos, having had a divine father but a mortal mother, and so was an appropriate figure for human nothoi to gather around (and demonstrate their worth as akin to that of Heracles).

It was to this gymnasium that Themistocles invited "noble-born" fellow citizens of his own age to join him in exercise, hoping, according to Plutarch, to minimize still further the lingering social distance between those recently enfranchised as Athenian citizens and those of the old noble citizen families.[2] It was here too, no doubt, that he heard and exchanged the latest news, including about the destruction of Phaleron by the Aeginetans.

His exercising in the gymnasium must also be understood as no simple leisure pursuit. It was a fundamental activity of any free-born man and active citizen of his city. Just like attending the palaistra while growing up, exercising in the gymnasium as an adult was a way to demonstrate one's skill and strength and thus ability (ultimately to defend one's city in wartime). It was also a way to continue to compete with fellow citizens for honor, supremacy, and renown, and to develop the mind and understanding, not to mention strengthen connections and networks, through conversations with others from similar socioeconomic backgrounds. The ideal was that citizens should not have to spend their time working for a living but, owing to their slaves, their family wealth, and/or their successful business interests, could afford to dedicate their time to self-improvement in the gymnasium and, equally important, to the business of being an active citizen of the polis, taking part in its political, legal, and military activities. Time spent in the gymnasium was thus time spent developing the experience, reputation, and connections needed for an active public life.

In this period, against the backdrop of continued uncertainty for Athens and, indeed, the destruction wrought on its port by Aegina, Themistocles had been not only exercising in the gymnasium but seeking to make connections in a number of different spheres. We are told that he had formed a pederastic relationship with the older "beautiful Stesileos," a native of Ceos, resident in Athens.[3] This kind of relationship was nothing out of the ordinary in Athens: a young citizen male was expected to enter into a relationship with an older male citizen, and the relationships varied in nature from the purely intellectual to emotional and physical. The older male citizen was known in ancient Greek as the *erastes* (lover) – hence the term "pederastic" as the *erastes* of the *pais* (boy), – and the younger male, normally in his mid- to late teens, was known as the *eromenos* (beloved). Such relationships were intended to act as an important element of a young citizen's education and development, and they were crucial to forming the proper values of loyalty and honor, as well as an aversion to dishonor, within society. Given the educative value of the relationship, the boundaries of what was permissible within a pederastic relationship were also closely regulated within ancient society. At no point, for instance, was a pederastic relationship intended to overlap with the kind of money-for-sexual-pleasure exchange that characterized engagement with a prostitute. Indeed, young citizens found guilty of selling their bodies for sex were subsequently barred from active political service, as it was believed that anyone who would sell his own body would in turn be willing to betray his polis, the wider body politic.

Also around the time that Athens was weighing up military action in retaliation against Aegina, Themistocles seems to have attached himself to a philosopher for further training after his school years. Plutarch believes that the man Themistocles chose was from the same trittys as he, and that he specialized not in rhetoric but in *sophia,* wisdom. According to Plutarch the practice of sophia was in reality the practice of mixing natural intelligence with political dexterity. It was the art of being successful in civic life.[4]

Despite the precocious intelligence he displayed during his school years (and indeed perhaps because of it), Themistocles does not, according to the ancient sources, seem to have immediately taken the lessons of his new philosophical guide to heart. He was, according to Plutarch, "inconsistent" and "unstable," unable to tame his natural instincts with reason and training, and as a result veering from one wild course of action to another. Other ancient writers, such as Cornelius Nepos, argue that this period of wildness, in which Themistocles not only failed to control his natural instincts, but also lived extravagantly and took no care of his property, brought such disgrace not only on him but also on his father that Neocles was forced to act. In fact several ancient sources discuss the possibility that Neocles took the ultimate action of seeking to formally disinherit his son. The imagined declarations of both Neocles and Themistocles made up by the later rhetorician Libanius focus heavily on this issue of disinheritance. In Neocles' imagined speech, composed by Libanius, the father defends his decision on the grounds that Themistocles' actions irritated his friends and encouraged their enemies, bringing shame on the whole family. Neocles speaks of the sadness he felt, after having "shouted, raged, threatened, and groaned" at Themistocles to mend his ways, at being forced to formally request that a disinheritance be recognized in the courts of Athens, and he puts the blame for his actions entirely on Themistocles' shoulders. His fellow Athenians, he argues, sympathized with him and agreed that he had no other course of action left.[5]

Themistocles, of course, in Libanius's reply oration, presents a different picture, of a father who was never satisfied with Themistocles' achievements even as a young schoolboy, a man who set an impossibly high bar of expectation and was unjustly furious when it was not met. Neocles, according to Libanius's Themistocles, could not understand that boys, and indeed young men, will be boys, and that his antics were normal. Instead of showing toleration or reacting with the normal rage and annoyance that fathers feel against their wayward young sons, Neocles has reacted completely out of proportion by moving to have Themistocles disinherited. Such was the shock with which his mother reacted to the news that she fell down on her knees and pleaded with Neocles to disinherit her too, or kill her, rather than let her live with him as disinheritor of their son.[6]

This is all good rhetorical imaginative stuff, which not every ancient commentator believed had its roots in reality. In the first century CE Plutarch had argued that although Themistocles clearly had his wild years, the idea that his father formally disinherited him was not credible. Plutarch also sought to rebuff the idea—clearly well discussed in antiquity—that Themistocles' mother killed herself out of grief at the disinheritance. Instead he argued that Themistocles himself looked back on this period of enthusiasm unbridled by reason as a natural part of his development. Even the wildest young horses, Plutarch had Themistocles comment, make excellent steeds if they are properly trained and disciplined.[7] Could there be any better comment on the need to understand the nurture a person received than to point to his nature as giving him everything he needed for success? Themistocles was being influenced, trained, and disciplined by the people he chose to surround himself with and by the unsettling, uncertain, and tumultuous events that were taking place in and around the city of Athens during his teens and twenties. Together these different elements were offering insights into what was possible within the Athenian system, the balance that needed to be maintained between strong leadership and the perception of freedom if individuals wanted to have an impact, and how to position oneself and maintain that balance through hard work, social connections, and political dexterity. But no doubt the circumstances of his upbringing had also left something deeper: a need for control and power over his own destiny in response to almost a decade of extreme uncertainty, fear, and societal change.

At some point in the early 490s, Themistocles seems to have finally taken on board that training and discipline. Some ancient sources portray the shock of disinheritance as what led Themistocles to mend his ways, others see it as a more gradual process of growing up as he moved into his mid-twenties. Themistocles now began to live modestly, to refrain from overindulgence, and to focus all his energies on one thing: politics. Plutarch suggests that his father tried to warn him off, taking him down to the coastline to point out all the old Athenian warships that had been abandoned and neglected on the shore when they had stopped being useful, as a metaphor for the way Athens tended to fetter and then cut dead its political leaders when they no longer were able to maintain that crucial balance between strong leadership and political freedom. But it seems Themistocles was not to be dissuaded, not so much because he wanted to do good for the city of Athens as because, at least according to his later biographers, he wanted to be renowned for performing great deeds.[8]

He was of course not the only young man who – in the heady decade after Cleisthenes' reforms and the opening up of the political system at Athens – wanted to make his mark. And in many ways Themistocles remained at a huge disadvantage. Despite the fact that Athens's system now embodied isonomia and had broken up the old power networks of the elite aristocratic families through its new system of demes, trittyes, and tribes, those families were still present in Athens. They were still wealthy, which meant that the male family members were well educated and practiced in rhetoric and thus able to make their points heard convincingly in the city's new governing council chamber, or at the grand democratic assembly on the Pnyx hill, or in the law courts, or even in the street. More than their current wealth, they also had a wealth of history behind them: their families had been at the heart of Athenian politics for, in some cases, centuries; their ancestors had performed great deeds. These things counted when the current generation of these families stood up to speak.

Against such advantages Themistocles had little to show: no particular family wealth, no family history of great deeds, and of course the lingering sense of inferiority from his being such a newly enfranchised Athenian citizen. We hear in the sources that on occasion he sought to act like one of the young men of great lineage and wealth: he invited a famous lyre player to practice at his house so that people would visit regularly just as they did the houses of the elites. On other occasions, he even tried to compete directly with them. One of the up-and-coming young men of the era was Cimon, son of Miltiades. Miltiades had been archon of the city in the year Themistocles was born (and his father may have followed Miltiades back from Thrace at that time). But this was only the beginning of Cimon's family heritage. Miltiades' father was Cimon "Coalemos" (Simpleton)—a man who had been victorious multiple times in the chariot races at the Olympic Games, who was eventually murdered by Hippias and Hipparchus out of jealousy over his ongoing Olympic victories. And Cimon Coalemos's grandfather, also called Miltiades, had been archon of

Athens in the first half of the seventh century BCE. So when the young Cimon splashed his cash around the Olympic Games, setting up fine tents with magnificent furnishings and hosting lavish banquets, people thought the extravagance was in keeping with his family heritage – especially at the Olympics, the scene of his grandfather's many successes. When Themistocles tried to outdo Cimon in extravagance at the Olympics, people thought he was exalting himself far beyond his position and acting like a pretentious upstart.

Another of the young men at Athens with whom Themistocles sought to compete in this period was Aristides. This rivalry was slightly different. Both were from fairly modest backgrounds, Aristides five years or so older than Themistocles. Their rivalry, we are told, stemmed from the fact that they were both, when young, in a pederastic relationship with the same older man (the "beautiful Stesileos"), and from their jealousy of one another in competing for Stesileos's affections there grew a lifelong political enmity. Added to this was Aristides' slight age advantage over Themistocles, which meant that he was already a full adult citizen at the time of great reforms of Cleisthenes in 508/7. Aristides was said to have been a close friend of Cleisthenes and as a result to have been in the political limelight ever since. He had gained a reputation for steadfastness and adherence to justice, and as someone who always told the truth. Moreover, he was said to have been, despite his own modest background, a supporter of the continued influence of the aristocracy in government, and so a welcome friend of Athens's elites. This, for the ancient commentators, put Aristides on a collision course with Themistocles both in terms of character (Themistocles was often portrayed as dexterous, reckless, and impetuous) and in terms of political sympathies (Themistocles always favored giving more power to the wider populace).[9]

The one thing Aristides and Themistocles do seem to have agreed on – at least in the early days – was that Athens should not make itself a vassal of Persia. Athens had flirted with Persia in the immediate aftermath of Cleisthenes' reforms and the ejection of Isagoras and the Spartan king, when the city was surrounded by Greek city-states keen to put Athens back in its place. But now the Persian King was issuing demands that Athens should take back the aging Hippias as its tyrant ruler – something both Aristides and Themistocles, as well as a majority of Athenians, did not want to see happen.

The Persian King was not about to wage war against Athens for this reason alone – but what did make Athens a target was the subsequent involvement of the Athenians with a rebellion against him on the Asia Minor coast of the Aegean. At the turn of the fifth century, the people of the island of Naxos had rebelled against their aristocratic rulers in an effort, some claimed, to emulate the achievements of the Athenians in introducing isonomia. On the coast of Asia Minor, the ruler of the city of Miletus, a man called Aristagoras, offered himself and his forces to the Persian King to reestablish aristocratic rule on Naxos (and at the same time assert Persian control over the island). Darius had agreed and sent his own general and troops to fight alongside Aristagoras. But the attempted takeover of the island of Naxos proved a disaster, and Aristagoras, sure that he was to be made the scapegoat for the whole venture, now, in an extraordinary volte-face, declared himself inspired by the Naxian (as well as Athenian) example and a convert to "people power." As such, he sent ambassadors up and down the Aegean coast of Asia Minor encouraging them to follow him in a revolt against the Persian King himself.

The bigger question was, What would Athens do? Aristagoras himself came to the Assembly place of the Athenian people, on the

Pnyx hill, to make his case. This was the beating heart of the Athenian system. All male citizens had the right to attend the Assembly, and any citizen, as well as those who came on official business to the city of Athens, had the right to speak. Speakers had to make themselves heard across a crowd of thousands (who themselves were unlikely to have been completely silent) and to convince that crowd with their own words of their point of view. Each citizen then voted on the issue – probably through a show of hands. It was a system based entirely on the speaker's ability to sway the people, as he looked out over the thousands of faces that stared back at him with no doubt a mixture of interest, derision, anger, support, and indifference. We do not know whether Themistocles and Aristides were in the Assembly that day, listening to Aristagoras make his case, but it seems likely that such keen young men, with political ambitions, were there.

On one hand, Aristagoras played down the might of the Persian army. But on the other, he played up the ancestral links among his hometown, Miletus, the wider community of peoples along the Aegean coast of Asia Minor, and the Athenians. He underlined the Athenian inspiration for the actions of Naxos and now himself and others. The Athenian Assembly – likely with Themistocles and Aristides among them – listened intently. Athens was less than a decade old in its new system of isonomia. It had managed spectacular victories against the ring of Greek foes that had surrounded it just six years earlier. Soldiers who had fought in those battles were no doubt in among the group gathered in the Assembly, standing as testament to Athens's power and might. The Assembly voted to join the rebellion. Twenty warships were dispatched from Athens to the Asia Minor coast.

Over the next five years, between 499 and 494, the revolt against the Persian King struggled for momentum. Initially the

Athenians, along with their allies, had successfully made their way to the Persian satrapal capital city of Sardis, pillaging and burning across the city. But then the slower Persian war machine began to crank into full action, and Persian forces poured into the area, forcing the Athenians to retreat. Before long the Athenian ships had sailed home again. In 496/5, the archon in Athens was Hipparchus, a relation of the Peisistratid tyrant family. He now advocated peace with Persia – but it came a little too late. Persian forces were bearing down on Miletus, the stronghold of Aristagoras, and the rebellion had been completely extinguished, following a major defeat at sea, by 494.

One of the other people who had answered Aristagoras's call in 499 was Miltiades, the man who had been archon in Athens when Themistocles was born. Miltiades had set off from the Chersonesus to capture the north Aegean islands of Lemnos and Imbros, which Athens had historically laid claim to. He was successful, but, following the failure of the revolt in 494, Miltiades knew that the game was up, and it was only a matter of time before the Persian King came for him. He set sail with his wife, his son Cimon, and all his worldly possessions for Athens. It was one of life's ironies that when Miltiades came back to Athens in 493, the man who was about to become archon was Themistocles.[10]

CHAPTER FOUR

Calling the Shots

When the Athenians gathered for their great annual festival in honor of Dionysus, most probably in the year that Themistocles held the archonship and Miltiades returned to Athens, one of the tragedians chosen to compose plays for the festival was a man called Phrynichus. He was already well known, having composed plays for the festival for more than fifteen years. Yet now he brought a play before the Athenian audience titled *The Capture of Miletus*. This was no tragedy based in the mythical past. This was a historical tragedy, putting on the stage the story of the sack of the city of Miletus which had occurred just the year before. Although the city's destruction had not happened on Athens's doorstep, the tale of the downfall of Miletus hit the Athenians hard. Miletus had begun life as a colony founded by Athens. And Athens had also been very much involved in the Ionian Revolt and particularly in the carnage and destruction inflicted on the Persian-controlled city of Sardis.

We are told by Herodotus that Phrynichus's play struck such a nerve that the production was stopped and he was put on trial and fined for reminding the Athenians of their "domestic" (*oikia*) misfortunes; his play was also banned from ever being performed again. Such a harsh punishment for writing a play underlines how central dramatic performance had become to Athenian culture. Theater was not sideline "entertainment" to engage in during down time. Watching plays in the Theater of Dionysus as part of the city-wide religious festival in honor of the god, was an absolutely critical experience for the whole polis, as well as for those coming to the city from across the Greek world, who gathered together to reflect on the nature of the Athenian state and its fortunes.[1]

Phrynichus's trial was not the only one in Athens that year. The recent arrival of Miltiades and his family back in the city also reminded the Athenians of the Ionian Revolt and its ultimate failure. But there was more to the history than that. Miltiades, despite his efforts to help the Ionian Revolt, had spent the majority of his last decades ruling like a tyrant in the Chersonesus. Given Athens's strong steps away from tyranny and toward isonomia and empowerment of its people, Miltiades and his family must have looked very out of place indeed.

Whether people were truly concerned about Miltiades' recent activities, or whether more trifling concerns were enflamed by other elite aristocratic families, such as the Alcmaeonids, who saw this as an opportunity to reignite old inter-elite rivalries, we are not sure. But soon after Miltiades returned to Athens, he was put on trial for his tyranny in the Chersonesus.

Themistocles was thirty-one years old and held the position of "eponymous archon," one of nine archons elected annually, with responsibility for heading up the civic governance of the city. (Other archons were responsible for military and religious leadership.) He had just reached the minimum age to hold the post; a candidate had to be thirty or older, as well as a citizen in good standing, for which there was a preliminary examination. Indeed, it is testimony to how far he had come during the early 490s in terms of being seen as a citizen in good standing that he had been voted into this office so quickly after becoming eligible. Plutarch comments that, as part of his ascent, Themistocles had held the office of "water commissioner" in Athens and commemorated his tenure by setting up a bronze statue of a female water carrier, paid for with the fines collected from infringements of the water regulations. (We also presume that at some point in his twenties, he had married. Plutarch tells us Themistocles was married to a woman called Archippe, a daughter of an Athenian citizen named Lysander from the deme of Alopece, located just outside the city walls of Athens. We know he had a number of sons with Archippe. At some stage in his life, he remarried, to a woman whose name is unknown – nor do we know what happened to Archippe – and went on to have several daughters as well.)[2]

But despite the experience and insight Themistocles seems to have gained through his twenties – from the people he chose to associate with and learn from; from the knowledge that came from trying (and sometimes failing) both to blur the social distinctions within Athenian society and to compete directly with the traditional elites; and from the lessons learned while watching the rough-and-tumble of Athenian politics and observing the importance of maintaining a critical balance in Athenian public life in order not to end up cast aside like an abandoned ship left to rot – it was a big step from water commissioner to archon. Themistocles was still young and still had a lot to learn.

Moreover simply being archon did not mean that he alone was calling the shots in Athens. We have seen already that many decisions were made by the demos, the citizens of Athens as a group, in their Assembly on the Pnyx, and votes on crucial issues were taken by a show of hands following speeches from a number of speakers. Assemblies, however, did not take place every day (we think there were about forty meetings a year). On other occasions decisions came to the Boule – the five hundred citizens elected by lot from across the citizen body to serve for one year as the governing council of the city. The council dealt with most of the day-to-day business of the city (as well as deciding the agenda for the Assembly), and an even smaller group, known as the *prytaneis*, composed of fifty council members selected on a rotating basis from among the Boule, was kept on permanent standby to take immediate decisions in times of need. Alongside these bodies was the Areopagus. This group – named after the hill on which the group met in central Athens – claimed for itself the role of guardian of the city's laws, purportedly stretching back into Athens's mythical past. It had no regularly changing membership or fixed representation from each tribe. Instead it was composed of former archons and thus had a weighty number of the city's traditional aristocratic families as members.

Nor was this the full extent of officials in positions to exert authority within the still evolving Athenian political system. Since 501 BCE, ten military generals had been elected each year to represent each of the ten tribes of Athens and lead the Athenians in battle, but they were also respected voices in decision making because of their seasoned experience on the battlefield and elsewhere. And alongside them were the nine elected archons. In addition to the archons and generals, there were also boards of treasurers, who had responsibility for different key funds across Athens. And while Athens had no civil service or government bureaucracy, an increasingly large number of officials were elected into numerous posts year after year to run different aspects of the city's business (and eventually its empire). By the second half of the fifth century, there would be some seven hundred officials with domestic responsibilities elected each year, and the same number again with duties outside Attica across the empire. As eponymous archon Themistocles was thus just one cog in an increasingly complex machine of government. And in the case of Miltiades, it was the court of the Areopagus that now held his fate in their hands, as they were the people in charge of his trial.

The case for the prosecution was fairly clear—Athens had ousted its own tyrant and was now a place of isonomia. It was no home for former tyrants and certainly not for those who might want to be so again. But what about the defense? Themistocles would have been present to hear Miltiades make his case: he had been appointed to his post by the Athenians, over non-Athenians. He had on the surface followed in the service of the Great King but had secretly worked to undermine Persia's military expeditions. He had joined the Ionian Revolt against the Persian King and had taken control of the islands of Lemnos and Imbros, which he now gave as gifts to Athens.

Perhaps Miltiades also asked the Athenians, and particularly the members of the Areopagus, to think about what was coming next. Herodotus would later make it clear that on hearing of the destruction of the sanctuaries at Sardis, the Persian King had had to ask who the Athenians were. Incensed on hearing that they had once promised fealty but then joined the revolt against him and had had the temerity to ransack the sanctuaries of his Lydian subjects, he is said to have fired an arrow into the sky and prayed for the right to rain down punishment on the Athenians. His chief courtier was instructed to repeat three times to him every day at dinnertime, "Remember the Athenians." The clock was ticking. Darius was preparing to come for Athens. And when he did, Miltiades perhaps reminded the Areopagus court, would it not be useful to have someone in their midst who had intimate knowledge of Persian military tactics and strength, and who could thus help Athens survive?[3]

Miltiades was acquitted by the Areopagus. And indeed, rather than slinking off into the shadows as a free man, he was soon after elected to be one of Athens's military generals – a position to which he would be reelected each year until his death.[4] It seems that the people of Athens were only too well aware of their need for experienced defenders of their newfound isonomia – and were willing to take those with the requisite experience even if they also had a whiff of tyranny about them. Here was another lesson for Themistocles: even in such a difficult situation, Miltiades had turned the tables by arguing his usefulness and worth to the Athenians. The game of Athenian politics was as much about need as it was about principles.

Yet as well as riding the uncertain waves of Athenian political intrigue, Themistocles may have used his time as archon in 493/2 to set out his sense of the direction in which Athens needed to move – and that direction chimed with Miltiades' focus on Athens's need to defend itself. For Thucydides later commented that the building and fortifying of the Piraeus port at Athens, whose completion Themistocles would oversee in the early 470s, had begun life as a building project much earlier when Themistocles had held formal office (which most historians take to mean his archonship).[5]

To be sure, the case for Athens to upgrade its current port, Phaleron, by moving its merchant and military operations to the west, to the small coastal community of Piraeus, which had three natural harbors, made sense. Athens's ongoing struggles with Aegina, and the fact that the Aeginetans had raided and destroyed Phaleron in living memory, would have provided good enough incentive to the Athenians to improve their port facilities – and with that to enlarge their fleet. But the possibility of a Persian attack, perhaps in league with the Aeginetans and who knew which other Greek cities, would have made the idea of an enlarged and defensible port that could accommodate and protect both grain and other merchant supply ships, as well as a bigger Athenian fleet, even more enticing. Not to mention the fact that such a construction project, along with the ongoing work that would be needed to build, supply, maintain, and man the enlarged Athenian fleet, would provide employment for a vast number of the Athenian demos for some time to come. Overall, the proposal thus sounds like a real crowd-pleaser.

Yet this was still a massive change in Athenian planning and activity: a move from focusing firmly on Athens's land-based military might to investing in future seaborne power, and thus also a change from a reliance on men who could afford the armor of the hoplite foot soldiers (the middle classes) and the armor and trained horses of the cavalry (the aristocracy) to those who could build and row warships (any able-bodied man). At stake was a widening of the group on whom Athens relied for its defense – a widening to involve the whole demos. No doubt such a plan would have met with resistance from elites who saw advantage for themselves in being the people on whom Athens had to rely for its defense: after all, it made sense that those who defended the city had the most right to have a decisive say in its running.

It is thus a lot to lay at the thirty-one-year-old Themistocles' door as something that he alone, while archon for a single year, as a single cog in the complex Athenian political machinery managed to convince the Athenians to do. He may well have supported the idea, but if planning for a new large port at Piraeus and the building of a bigger fleet did begin as early as 493/2, it is likely to have arisen out of a wider sense among a wider percentage of Athens's elites, its trading classes, and the mass of the people that it was a sensible (and at least for some levels of Athenian society desirable) next step.

However, the Athenians also had more pressing matters to attend to than a massive port- and fleet-expansion project. In the same year that Themistocles was archon and Miltiades returned to Athens and was put on trial, representatives from the Persian Great King arrived in Athens – just as Miltiades had suggested at his trial that they would one day. The Persian King, they related, had sent messengers to all the Greek islands of the Aegean as well as the major mainland Greek cities. The question asked of each one of them was simple: Did they submit to the Great King or not? To submit, they must make offerings of earth and water from their city. All the Aegean islands that had been asked had submitted. Even Athens's great island rival Aegina had submitted. Thebes – Athens's nearest mainland rival – would later claim to have been the first mainland city to offer its submission. What would Athens do?

We are told that two people took the lead in the argument within Athens about how to respond: Miltiades and Themistocles. Miltiades, flush from the success of defending himself in the court of the Areopagus and with his personal knowledge of dealing with the Persian King, was an obvious candidate to take a prominent role in the discussions. Themistocles was an archon, and so too an important voice, despite his young age. Yet he had hitherto no experience in dealing with the Persians, and certainly no direct experience of the Great King. What is perhaps surprising is that, according to the ancient sources, it was Themistocles who suggested the Athenians make the harshest response. Whereas Miltiades proposed that the heralds should be executed, Themistocles insisted that both they and their interpreter should be put to death – since the interpreter was just as guilty for the message he translated as the heralds were for bringing it to Athens in the first place.[6]

Putting heralds to death was an unheard-of response – they were messengers and thus generally sacrosanct and under the protection of the gods. Athens could simply have refused their request for submission and sent them on their way. Instead, the Athenians chose to make a clear, and irreversible, statement of their attitude toward the Great King. Herodotus later reported that the Persian heralds were cast into a pit ("earth") by the Athenians and left to die. That Miltiades had advocated this course of action was perhaps understandable: he had been found not guilty of treason but may well have been anxious, in the immediate aftermath of his trial, to portray himself unmistakably as no friend of the Persian King. Taking a hitherto unthinkably violent line on how to respond to the Persian heralds was one very clear way of doing that.

But why was Themistocles so eager to break the boundaries of the "divine" respect normally owed to heralds – and indeed, to do so in an even more stark way than Miltiades? Was it youthful exuberance? Was it born of Themistocles' desire to make a name for himself as an up-and-coming member of Athenian society? Was it a response, perhaps, to his own concerns about his more borderline status as a citizen and his desire to show himself a die-hard Athenian? Was it a statement of how much Themistocles believed in, and wanted to protect, the system of isonomia that had been born just as he had come of age, and in which he had matured to adulthood? Or was it, perhaps, a realistic response to the fact that the Persian King was already intent on destroying Athens, and so Athens might as well make a show of strength? We cannot be sure. But what is clear is that Themistocles' involvement in agitating for such an unparalleled reaction to the heralds' request for earth and water made it impossible for Darius to do anything except launch a full-blown attack on Athens. Themistocles and Miltiades – in persuading the people of Athens to follow them – had sealed Athens's fate.

At the beginning of the spring of 492, Darius put his nephew Mardonius in charge of an army and a fleet, tasked with exacting revenge on all those involved in the Ionian Revolt, attacking Athens and the neighboring Euboean city of Eretria, and conquering as much of mainland Greece as he could. The fleet sailed round the coast of the Aegean and made it as far as the Mount Athos peninsula before being caught in a powerful storm. Herodotus writes that three hundred ships were destroyed and their crews eaten by "savage creatures" of the sea. The land army got as far as Macedon, where the king, Alexander (not "the Great"), offered submission to the Persian ruler. But it too faced a setback when the camp was attacked at night by a wild Thracian tribe, which wounded Mardonius himself. Mardonius eventually managed to restore order and the army got as far south as the boundaries of Macedon and Thessaly.[7]

We know little of the men who succeeded Themistocles in 492 and 491 as eponymous archon, and none of the ancient sources records either of them making any particular impact on Athens's foreign policy in the period. The Athenians would have been only too aware of Mardonius's advances and his setbacks. But it made no sense for them to march out to defend the city outside their own territory when so much of Greece had surrendered to the Persian heralds. There was only one thing to do: wait.

In spring 490 the two new commanders of the Persian forces, Datis and Artaphernes (a brother of Darius), gathered a fleet which they intended to use to transport horses and soldiers not up and around the northern coastline of the Aegean, as Mardonius had done, but directly across the heart of the sea to secure key islands in the Cyclades before landing on the east coast of mainland Greece. There was no mistaking their particular end goal. Plato later recounted that the Persian King had told his generals, "Come back with the Eretrians and the Athenians, if you want to keep your head."[8] Eretria was the main polis of the island of Euboea. The Eretrians were originally Ionians, like the Athenians, and had joined the Athenians in sending ships to aid the Ionian Revolt in 499; they had also been involved, along with the Athenians, in the destruction of Sardis. It was no surprise that they were thus top – alongside Athens – on Darius's hitlist.

The size of the Persian forces approaching Athens and Eretria in 490 is something that has vexed historians for generations. Herodotus tells us that six hundred triremes sailed in the Persian fleet. Later writers offer figures of between two hundred thousand and six hundred thousand men! Modern estimates suggest something more in the range of twenty thousand soldiers with perhaps a thousand horses and the rowing crews and supplies needed to transport them.[9] Regardless of the figure, it was a daunting force.

The Persian flotilla headed west, stopping to demand submission from the inhabitants of Rhodes and Naxos, before making a grandiose gesture of devotion on the island of Delos. The Persian commanders summoned the inhabitants of this sacred island, the birthplace of Apollo and Artemis, and told them that their King had instructed them to spare the island, and indeed honor it. They then produced 7½ tons of frankincense to burn on the altars in the gods' honor. This was a classic carrot-and-stick tactic: we offer honor to your gods but vengeance if you defy us – all we request is your submission and support. The islands of the Cyclades fell like dominoes, without the need for the Persians to leave troops behind to secure them. The island of Paros even contributed a trireme (the new ship of the line) to the Persian forces.

The people of Athens would have been well aware of each step of the Persians' approach up to the day their forces arrived at Eretria and prepared to besiege the brave citizens who had barricaded themselves in their city. For six days the siege was, Herodotus later recounted, "fierce."[10] But on the seventh, two Eretrians seem to have betrayed their city and enabled the Persians to infiltrate it. The Persians burned and looted the sanctuaries and enslaved the survivors, leaving them under guard, as they prepared to move on to the territory of Athens.

There was an old man among the Persian high command, now near his eighties: Hippias. This son of Peisistratus, who had once been tyrant of Athens until he was forced out by the Spartans, subsequently tried to have himself reinstalled as tyrant by the Spartans. Since that time he had been living in forced retirement in the Chersonesus. He was now the adviser to the Persian King and to the commanders of the Persian forces preparing to attack Athens. Perhaps he believed that even at his advanced age he would be put back in charge of the city after it submitted.

The Persian commanders sent messengers giving the Athenians once last chance to surrender. No doubt the Athenians had been debating what to do at this moment for weeks. They had roughly ten thousand hoplites as well as light-armed troops. Their call for support from other Greek city-states had resulted in only the small nearby polis of Plataea sending a thousand hoplites. Sparta had said it would come to help in due course.

Miltiades was one of the ten Athenian generals elected to represent Athens's tribes. Aristides, Themistocles' political rival, was another. Some commentators suggest that Themistocles too had been elected a general to represent his tribe but the evidence is unclear. As a board of ten they were overseen by the *polemarch* – elected as the archon of the army – a man called

Callimachus. Their first decision was whether to go out to fight the Persians wherever they landed or prepare for a siege of the city. Miltiades made the motion before the Athenian Assembly that as soon as they knew where the Persians were intending to land, every able-bodied man, including slaves, who would be given their freedom in return for fighting for Athens, should leave the city to meet the Persians in battle.

Miltiades' plan was agreed to. Watchers along the coast passed information back through relays about the movement of the Persian fleet as it set sail from Euboea. Would it go to Phaleron, as the Aeginetans had done, or elsewhere? Soon the ships were spotted sailing north along the Attic coast. They were heading for Marathon, the place where Hippias's father, Peisistratus, had once landed with his own troops to make himself tyrant of Athens and where Hippias's family had owned land.

The Athenians began their march to Marathon to rendezvous with their Plataean allies. Pheidippides, a long-distance runner, was sent to Sparta to tell the Spartans that the time had come to send troops. He arrived in about thirty-six hours, having covered 150 miles, only to be told that the Spartans, for religious reasons, could not send troops until the time of the full moon. He ran back to Marathon to pass on to the generals the news that the Spartans would come – eventually. He also recounted that he had been visited by the god Pan during his run, who had said he would help the Athenians in the battle, spreading panic, if they offered him worship in return.

The Athenians were willing to give the gods anything for their support: Artemis was offered a sacrificed animal for every Persian killed. But ultimately there was a decision to make. The Athenians were now encamped on the southern side of the Plain of Marathon, in and around a sanctuary of Heracles. The Spartans had not yet arrived. But the longer the Athenians waited, the greater the chance that their morale would suffer and perhaps some would change sides, as had happened at Eretria, or that the Persians would find a way to encircle them. Half the generals wanted to attack. Half wanted to wait. We do not know which side Aristides or Themistocles took, but Miltiades was for attacking. The casting vote came down to the polemarch, Callimachus, who agreed with Miltiades.

Herodotus recounts that the Athenians waited several more days. The reason for the delay is unclear, some commentators arguing that the Athenians used the time to observe the Persian forces' daily rhythms and movements, so as to judge what was the best time of day to attack. Others focus on Miltiades himself. Despite there being a polemarch to oversee the generals, the Athenian tradition was for actual command of the army to rotate among all ten generals on a daily basis. Following their decision to fight, Herodotus tells us that each general whose day it was yielded his command to Miltiades, whom they all wanted to lead the Athenians and Plataeans in battle. But Miltiades did not give the command to attack until it was his official day in command. Did he simply want to ensure that the glory was his and his alone? Or by some fate, did something happen on his day of command that persuaded him that it was the right moment to attack? Scholars have argued, for instance, based on late ancient sources, that perhaps the key to his decision to attack that day was that the Persian cavalry was for some reason not immediately available to commit to the battle, which evened the odds for the Persian and Athenian/Plataean foot soldiers.[11]

We are told by Plutarch that both Aristides and Themistocles took up position in the center of the Greek battle line, where their respective tribes, of Leontis and Antiochis, were positioned. Some of the ancient commentators describe a gentlemen's agreement between Aristides and Themistocles to put aside their personal rivalry and stand shoulder to shoulder in support of one another against the Persians.[12] And of course it was not just the two of them who needed to fight in unison: they were fighting alongside their fellow tribesmen drawn from the different trittyes spilled across Attica. Moreover, standing in the center of the battle line they were faced with the hardest job of all. Miltiades had arranged the Greek line to be strongest at the wings, both to offer the chance of encircling the Persians and to prevent the Greeks from being encircled. But this left the center of the line thinner and more vulnerable.

Miltiades' battle plan, according to Herodotus, involved closing the distance between the Athenians and the Persians as quickly as possible. Hence, when the Greek line had advanced to just under a mile away from the Persians, the final battle sacrifices were made and Miltiades gave the command to "rush at them." The Athenians and Plataeans, Herodotus recounts, covered the last mile – eight stadia in ancient distance terms – at a run, or probably a jogtrot followed by a final sprint.[13] Such an achievement – running that distance in full armor while maintaining some kind of line and military discipline, mostly likely under a hail of Persian arrows – has bewitched scholars ever since. But the Athenians and Plataeans managed to close the distance and fall upon the Persians in hand-to-hand combat. As the comic poet Aristophanes would later put it, "the demos – the people – competed with the Medes [the Persians] in the sword-dance for the land at Marathon."[14]

Plutarch reports that both Themistocles and Aristides "fought brilliantly." They held the Greek center for at least several hours until the Greek wings, one led by Callimachus and the other by the Plataeans, had turned the Persian forces ranged against them and could regroup to support the by-then weakening Greek forces in the center line. Together they now pushed the Persians back toward the sea. Callimachus died in the fighting at the water's edge, as did another of the military generals, Stesileos. But Miltiades, Themistocles, and Aristides emerged unscathed as the Persians fled into their ships and set sail from Marathon.[15]

But the threat was not over. Herodotus mentions a shield signal coming to the Persians from Athenian territory, perhaps reminding them that they still had supporters inside the city. While Pheidippides, or perhaps another runner, was sent back to Athens to announce the victory (and famously dropped dead just after delivering his message), the Athenian forces en masse now also had to return to Athens in sufficient strength and sufficient good time to defend the city from the Persians if they chose to land at Phaleron. Plutarch claims that Aristides and his tribe stayed at Marathon to secure the Persian prisoners and captured loot. But Themistocles, along with Miltiades and the rest of the forces, marched back to Athens, where they prepared themselves once again for battle in the gymnasium of Cynosarges, Themistocles' gymnasium of choice in Athens as a nothos child. When the Persian fleet appeared off Phaleron, the commanders somehow got wind that the Athenian forces were back and ready to defend their city. The Persians decided not to land and instead melted away into the hazy-blue distance of the Aegean.[16]

Back at Marathon, Aristides was also in charge of cremating and honoring the Athenian dead. A special area was created for the funerary ritual of the 192 Athenians who had died; they were then cremated with all the religious ceremony and honor that could be mustered. A permanent memorial to their valor was created, with tombstones naming the 192, arranged by their tribe, on top of a memorial mound, which was seen by the ancient tour-guide writer Pausanias more than six hundred years later.[17] The Plataeans and former slaves who had died were buried separately but with equal honor. The Persians, however, were stripped and left rotting in the sun, to be later thrown into a pit – all 6,400 of them. The Spartans, arriving the day after the battle, saw the scale of the Athenian and Plataean victory. Nothing would be the same again.

CHAPTER FIVE

The Power of Exclusion

Nothing was the same for Themistocles, either. Plutarch reports that despite his role in the victory at Marathon, Themistocles reacted strongly to the discovery that many saw Miltiades as the hero of the hour. Themistocles, we are told, could not sleep for envy at the honor that Miltiades now claimed for himself, setting up a statue and sanctuary of Pan at Marathon and dedicating his own helmet at Olympia with an inscription pierced into its metal: "Miltiades dedicated [this] to Zeus." Themistocles was in return "forced out of his bed at night." He became "wrapped up in his own thoughts," "refused invitations to drinking parties," and told all who questioned his behavior that "the trophy of Miltiades" would not let him sleep. Plutarch put this down to two causes: first, Themistocles' own ambition and deep desire for fame, which was wounded by the fact that someone else was firmly fixed in the spotlight of Athenian honor and occupying the sweet spot in Athenian politics between strong leadership and empowering Athenian freedom. Second, more charitably, Plutarch suggested that Themistocles' detached status in the aftermath of Marathon could have been an early example of his long-sightedness and understanding that although the Persians might have disappeared across the Aegean, they would not be gone forever; he was already worrying about what to do if they came again. The reality is much more likely to have been the former than the latter.[1]

Indeed, Themistocles was not alone in Athens in resenting the honor given to Miltiades. After all, the tipping point between strong leadership and Athenian freedom was a perilously fragile one, and one that Miltiades soon himself overbalanced. Miltiades asked that a crown of olive branches be awarded to him as a symbolic recognition of his victory, at which another Athenian, Sophanes, stood up in the middle of the Assembly on the Pnyx to protest. When Miltiades had single-handedly defeated the Persians, Sophanes declared, he could have a crown. But Marathon was an Athenian victory by the people of Athens – not one man. The crowd, it is said, agreed with him. It was the people of Athens who chose to erect a new monument on the Acropolis in honor of their victory and simultaneously in honor, not of Miltiades, but of Callimachus, the dead polemarch, who, in the dedicating inscription, was said to have "fought at Marathon for all the Greeks."[2] At Delphi, the Athenians moved to construct a new treasury adorned with the heroic exploits of Heracles, the pan-Greek hero, and Theseus, who had been an early king of Athens (in his youth he killed the Cretan Minotaur) as well as the founder of important Athenian religious festivals such as the Panathenaia, and who thus represented a specifically Athenian hero. Alongside it they constructed a line of ten statues, each representing one of Athens's ten tribes, accompanied by an inscription: "The Athenians dedicate this to Apollo, first fruits from the Persians at the Battle of Marathon."[3] The message was clear: individuals might do great deeds, but they did them on behalf of the people of Athens, who collectively shared the glory. It was a new vision of people-powered victory and of the balancing act that all who sought to lead in Athens had to perform.

Plutarch tells us that Marathon, although unsettling for Themistocles because of the honor Miltiades was claiming for himself, did at least finally cure Themistocles of his former weaknesses – particularly overindulgence in wine and women. Perhaps it was the grim reality of the battle that made him more serious.[4] Or perhaps it was his acute longing – which kept him awake at night – to experience the kind of glory Miltiades was experiencing (or at least claiming for himself) that encouraged him to put aside his indulgences in pursuit of his goal.

The people of Athens wanted more too, drunk on the nectar of glorious victory. Yet there was a rub: they had denied Miltiades' claim to celebrate the victory at Marathon as his alone, rather than collectively theirs, but they needed an individual general with experience to lead them in search of further victories. Miltiades, despite his public snub, was elected general for another year, and he promised them another victory, this time taking the fight to the Persians. The Athenians took him at his word, voting him the money and manpower to take seventy ships on his venture – a venture he never fully revealed to the people, explaining that his target must remain top secret for fear of the Persians getting wind of it. It was another classic case of need and desire triumphing over principle in Athenian politics.

It also became a clear symbol of how quickly luck – or, rather, the gods' goodwill – could shift that within a few months of this expedition's setting sail, it was back at Phaleron in tatters. Miltiades, his knee broken and leg already gangrenous, was stretchered off his ship. Soon his old elite aristocratic family rivals started to gather like a pack of wolves scenting easy prey. Chief among them was a member of the Alcmaeonid family – the family which had been at loggerheads with the Peisistratids, helped bring about the revolution of isonomia, been long-term rivals of Miltiades' family the Philaids, and were as keen to reassert themselves as champions of the people as they had been in the time of Cleisthenes in 508.[5] The Alcmaeonids now accused Miltiades of being an enemy of the people: he had cost them money, lives, and pride, but secured no victories in turn. The blind trust put by Athens in his "secret plan" had been paid back with his "tyrannical" secrecy and leadership. Once a tyrant, always a tyrant. And now he should pay the ultimate price.

Less than a year after Miltiades led the Athenians to victory at Marathon over the Persians, he was – feverish, unable to walk and even to speak on his own behalf – on trial once more in the court of the Areopagus. And this time there would be no escape. The court, which included Themistocles as a former archon and thus de facto member, found him guilty of costing the city money and Athenians their lives, and, most crucial, of acting in a tyrannical manner. The prosecutor Xanthippus, who was married to an Alcmaeonid, called for execution as the only just punishment. Perhaps Miltiades' great victory at Marathon hung on just potently enough in the minds of the court members (including Themistocles) that they could not bring themselves to impose this sentence. Instead, Miltiades was fined fifty talents. A single talent was twenty-six kilograms of pure silver, enough to pay two hundred rowers for a month. Fifty talents was thus an enormous sum, perhaps the entire cost of the failed expedition. Miltiades was confined to the dark, cramped confines of Athens's jail until he could pay it. He died there of his wounds a few days later.

Themistocles would thus have been confronted with perhaps the clearest proof of the warning his father had given him about Athens's tendency to choose leaders and then cast them aside when it suited them. His education in Athenian politics had reached a new level: he became an eyewitness to, indeed participant in, the sloughing off of a man who had hitherto been lauded as an exalted hero and savior. Themistocles cannot have been in any doubt about what the stakes were for those who got the balancing act of Athenian politics wrong or, more fundamentally, failed to deliver what they had promised to the Athenian people, thus threatening Athens's developing reputation as the emerging power center of Greece. An Athenian leader had to succeed and succeed big – or else he would at best be cast aside and at worst be faced with draconian punishment.

Miltiades' sentence did not die with him: the fine – and jail time until it could be paid – passed to his twenty-one-year-old son Cimon. This young man now had to grow up very quickly indeed, reaching out to his friends and allies, people like Aristides, who had been elected as archon in 489, just as Cimon lost his father and started his jail time. Cimon was also supported by Callias, a member of another old elite family, who, despite the social, financial, and political cloud hanging over the Philaid family, chose to marry Cimon's sister.[6] Somehow – and some of the ancient sources indicate it was with financial assistance from these friends – Cimon managed to pay off this enormous debt and regain his freedom. With the help of Aristides, he even managed to patch up his family's relationship with the Alcmaeonids by marrying one of their own: Isodike, whose great-uncle was no less than Cleisthenes the reformer.

In many ways these old elite families had begun perhaps to realize the need to stick together, for times were changing once again. In 488/7, less than a year after these events took place, the city of Athens bore witness to a new political event: ostracism, with which Themistocles, as a prominent member of the Athenian political scene, would become all too familiar over the following decade.

Ostracism had been formally part of Athens's political constitution since the reforms of Cleisthenes in 508, but no one had ever activated it. In 488/7, however, things changed. The author of *Constitution of the Athenians,* often attributed to Aristotle, would later claim that the enforcement of ostracism began because "the people were in high courage," a mixture of ongoing pride in their unexpected victory over the Persians at Marathon and their newly enthusiastic desire to "throw off" the yoke of tyrants – or, in fact, anyone who looked and acted like, or indeed was vaguely related to, tyranny.[7] Hence the first victim of ostracism in ancient Athens was a man called Hipparchus, named after one of his relatives, the Hipparchus son of the tyrant Peisistratus and brother of the tyrant Hippias who had been killed by the Tyrannicides Harmodius and Aristogeiton in 514. Despite this heritage, the Hipparchus who was ostracized in 488/7 had lived in Athens all his life quite peaceably: he had even been elected archon in 496/5. But now he was an easy target, related as he was to the man who had not only been forced out of Athens following his tyrannical rule but had fought with the Persians against the Athenians at Marathon. If men like Miltiades were going to be condemned for their "tyrannical" leadership of Athens's fleet, then men like Hipparchus were doomed. While the Athenians had seemingly been willing to turn a blind eye to these descendants of tyrants over the twenty years since 508, they now viewed them as potential snakes in the nest.

The process of ostracism was twofold. First a vote would be held on the Pnyx by the entire male citizen population as to whether there was a majority desire to remove someone from Attica (to "ostracize" them). If the vote passed, then two months later the citizens would convene again in the Agora, at which time every citizen wrote the name of the person he wanted to see ostracized on an *ostrakon* (a broken sherd of pottery) and placed it secretly in an urn. The votes were counted, and, provided a quorum of six thousand people voted, the candidate attracting the most negative votes was given ten days to leave Attica for ten years, on the understanding that after that time, he could return without any further stigma and with his property intact. It was a system which could quickly remove those who represented causes the Athenians no longer supported or individuals they no longer wanted in their midst.

Over the next four years, until 484, the Athenians, having never held an ostracism vote during the first twenty years of their new political system of isonomia, held one every year. And each year, someone connected with the tyrants who had held sway in Athens, or who could be connected more widely as a supporter of Athens's enemies, was ostracized. In 487/6 the hammer fell on a man named Megacles. He was an Alcmaeonid, no friend of the Peisistratid tyrants, and even a nephew of the great reformer Cleisthenes. But the Alcmaeonids – despite their role in prosecuting Miltiades – could not escape suspicion that they might have secretly sought to aid the Persians at the time of Marathon. (Herodotus reports that some thought them responsible for the signal given to the Persians from Athens after the battle, which encouraged the Persians to sail to Athens to try again.) At the same time, it is clear that Megacles himself incurred a lot of ill-will from the people due to his lifestyle choices. A total of 4,647 ostraca have been found that call for Megacles' banishment in 487/6. A good number include not only his name but also a reason for the vote – and the overwhelming reason people wanted to ostracize Megacles was because of his elite status, ostentatious wealth, and luxurious lifestyle. He was a "horse keeper," "overly fond of money" and even an "adulterer."[8]

Such ostentation and love of luxury were perhaps thought to make it more likely he would sympathize with the traditionally luxurious Persians and thus be an enemy of Athens (a charge that echoed the longer-term accusation that the Alcmaeonids had aided the Persians at the time of the Battle of Marathon). But it was perhaps also – more widely – a sign that the demos of Athens had increasingly little time, admiration, or sympathy for ostentatious display. Megacles himself, however, does not seem to have been too harshly affected by his ostracism. A couple of years after he was ostracized, in 484, he went to the Olympic Games and entered his chariot, horses, and driver in the famed chariot race. His chariot won, and Megacles, as owner, was crowned the winner of the race. He celebrated by paying the praise poet Pindar to write a victory ode about him and his illustrious family! In it, Pindar, no doubt with Megacles' approval, pulls no punches. In the opening lines the glory of the Alcmaeonid family is shouted to the rooftops, and a thinly veiled reference to Megacles' ostracism is described as good deeds being repaid with envy.[9]

Ostracism was not the only way in which the quickly changing political atmosphere of Athens in the 480s manifested itself. In the great City Dionysia, where tragedies and satyr dramas had been performed in honor of the god Dionysus since the sixth century BCE, in 487/6, just one year after the first ostracism, a new form of theater was introduced: comedy. Now alongside the tragedies, which usually took stories from ancient myths and explored them in front of the full citizen body of Athens (as well as visitors from outside Athens), the audience had the chance to revel in plays which specialized in ridicule, farce, and slapstick. But this was no light relief – these plays poked directly at the leading figures of Athens's political scene, making fun of their antics, their reputations, and their lifestyles through thinly veiled caricatures on the stage. It was no coincidence that Athenian comedy quickly gave rise to a new term in ancient Greek: *komoidoumenoi,* "those made fun of in comedy." And the people who found themselves bearing the brunt of this mockery were the leading figures of many of the elite aristocratic families, who had to sit in the audience, taking their beating with a smile.

Nor were these the only assaults on the traditional aristocratic families and ways of doing things in Athens at this time. In the same year that comedy was introduced at the Dionysia and Megacles was ostracized for his love of luxury and sympathy with the Persians, the Athenians voted to cease holding elections for the archons and instead to pick them randomly, by lot, from a list of five hundred chosen by the people of Athens.[10] The Athenians were effectively cutting off the possibility that well-known, well-educated, and gifted speakers might persuade people to vote for them (at least for the archonship), and instead underlining their belief that a wide pool of potential candidates were equally worthy and capable of being appointed – leaving it to the gods to decide the winner by lot. Education, experience, and wealth could get a man onto the long list, but could do nothing further to propel him into the archonship.

If these changes in the political atmosphere had not been ominous enough, in 484/3, something even more momentous happened: the first ostracism, according to Aristotle, in which the accused was not linked to tyranny, or even to sympathy with the Persians. Instead, he was ostracized because, to the demos, he seemed to be too big for his boots. That person was Xanthippus, who had led the prosecution against Miltiades on his return from his failed expedition to take the fight to the Persians in 489. The man who had championed the people against this "tyrant," was, five years later, sent packing as someone the demos of Athens no longer wanted in their midst for no other reason than that they believed he was now too powerful.[11]

In many ways the sudden adoption of ostracism and the introduction of comedy and targeted ridiculing of powerful individuals were simply new ways in which the Athenians sought to manipulate the balancing act they demanded at the heart of their system: the desire for strong leadership that at the same time maintained the essence of political freedom. Previously they had course corrected through law courts and trials for treason (such as that of Miltiades); now the ability to course correct was being incorporated into their political and cultural structures. Everywhere Themistocles turned in the 480s, he would have seen the narrowing of the path that the would-be-powerful in Athenian society had to walk, and an increase in the distance they had to fall when they misstepped.

It is hard to overemphasize how intense the nature of Athenian politics was in the 480s. There are only ten recorded instances of ostracism in Athens in the entirety of the fifth century BCE, and half of them occur in the 480s, the first period in which the Athenians chose to use the process. Aristotle and other fourth-century BCE as well as later writers characterized the arrival of ostracism as a symbol of the development of the people's belief in their own autonomy, the arrival of "people power." And no doubt, especially when combined with the other elements of political change we have seen – the change of the archonship to election by lot and the introduction of comedy – this was an important part of the picture.[12]

This rise in the Athenians' self-belief was also reflected in the physical landscape of the city during this time. Athens was rebuilt in the 480s to highlight its recent successes and the favor in which the gods held it, as well as its political system, which gave voice to the people. On the Acropolis, in the heart of Athens, a new temple to Athena had been built soon after the Athenians' political shakeup in 508 and their resultant military victories in 506. Now the Acropolis itself was remodeled and extended on its southern side to provide a wide, flat secure base for an even larger temple. The Athenians were remaking the very earth at the heart of their city to enable them to build even greater monuments to themselves and their gods. During the 480s, the new flat surface became the base for a temple that was the same size as the famed Parthenon, built later in the century on the site. Scholars think that this "pre-Parthenon" was half built—up to mid-column height—by 480/79, but it was never completed because of the return of the Persians. Yet the effort required to level and extend the Acropolis to provide the base for it, as well as the building that was completed, stands as testimony to how much the Athenians thought of themselves and their city in the 480s.[13]

The rising tide of people power does not fully explain why the 480s saw the introduction and prolific use of ostracism. What in particular did ostracism as a mechanism offer that made it suddenly so popular? Some historians have argued that it also became a handy tool for elite rivals to use against one another—the continuation of the elite rivalry that had defined Athenian politics for much of the previous century. In this version of events, ostracism became a civic tug of war between factions headed by particular individuals advocating particular policies, who utilized it as a strategic way of systematically eradicating their opponents. And in many cases, historians point to Themistocles as a prime manipulator of the ostracism votes in this period. Some have even argued that he was responsible for inventing the process, rather than making use of a system that was already part of the Athenian political constitution.[14]

It is easy to see why this theory seems attractive. Themistocles came from a non-aristocratic family, beginning life as a nothos of ambiguous status. He had as a result spent time on the margins of Athenian civic life, slowly making his way to the center of politics as an archon in the late 490s; he was a battle-proven leader after Marathon. He would have had a ringside seat in the Areopagus court for both of Miltiades' trials, and no doubt was a continuing voice in Athenian politics through the decade. He had much to gain to improve his own status within Athens from the rising empowerment of the people, and he probably had no great love for Athens's old aristocratic families, who bore the brunt of ostracism in this period. And he had clear anti-Persian and anti-tyranny credentials, not just from his valor on the battlefield at Marathon but from his call for the Persian heralds to be treated so harshly when they had arrived in Athens to demand the Athenians' submission. So if we were looking for a candidate who would take the lead in calling for the ostracism of people like Hipparchus, Megacles, and other "friends of the tyrants," Themistocles definitely fits the bill.[15]

But what this theory misses is the fact that Themistocles – as we know from the surviving ostraca – was as much the target of ostracism votes as other leaders. Ostracism votes in the 480s were not simply votes between two rival candidates – multiple candidates were often voted for in large numbers in any one ostracism procedure. In the ostracism vote that resulted in Megacles being banished in 487/6, we know of nine candidates who received votes, including Themistocles, Cimon, Callias, Xanthippus, Themistocles' philosopher-guru Mnesiphilus, and Themistocles' longtime rival and battle compatriot, Aristides. Themistocles was clearly attracting votes for his own ostracism among others; there just were not enough (in the 480s at least) to send him into exile.[16]

We thus need to imagine Athens in the 480s as a highly charged political environment in which there were simultaneously a huge upswell of pride from recent accomplishments, ongoing suspicions about particular families, and allegiances tied to increasingly divisive, shifting rivalries among different factions and their individual "leaders," as well as a wide range of views on the actions of individuals and on the political issues of the day, all of which could potentially lead to outbreaks of violence, political stasis (civil strife), or simply deadlock. Ostracism offered a unique way to respond to flashpoint issues on a case-by-case basis by removing from the debate the voice that attracted the most number of votes. It allowed a situation to be defused and deadlock (or worse: political stasis and the potential return of tyranny) to be avoided, while at the same time making it clear that it was the demos as a whole that governed Athens. Ostracism offered a way to maintain the balancing act of Athenian politics within an increasingly complex political and social environment.

Far from being a system that could be manipulated by one group or another, or indeed utilized in a strategic way to slowly eliminate rivals one by one, ostracism was an unpredictable process, which swung the axe down on individuals depending on the very particular circumstance of the day. In 487/6, Xanthippus received only a handful of ostracism votes. Within three years, in 484/3, he had been ostracized.[17] No one could predict, handle, or manipulate who would be ostracized. Themistocles was clearly a well-known and vocal individual at the center of a political system that had gone into overdrive during the 480s, with casualties at every turn. No one was safe – and that included Themistocles. His political life was not in any way assured of success. And yet his biographers make it clear that success was his prime goal. Themistocles had still to taste the kind of renown that Miltiades had ever so briefly enjoyed. The question was whether he could achieve it before losing his balance for good on the tightrope of Athenian politics.

CHAPTER SIX

Turning to the Sea

Not far from where Themistocles grew up, in the southern foot of Attica, was a place called Laurion. It was, and had long been, a working community, whose residents ran the tunnel mines of the area, processing and refining the silver that was painstakingly hacked free from the rock of the local mountainsides. The physical work was undertaken by a foreign slave population that faced perhaps the most backbreaking, unpleasant, and unglorifying task of any slaves in Athens.[1] By day and by night, aided only by the flicker of small, smelly oil lamps, slaves, often shackled, worked in tunnels big enough only to crawl along, following the shining seams of silver and lead as they twisted and turned through the rock. Their lungs choked and their eyes streaming with the dust of breaking rock, the hapless slaves had to hack away as best they could to release endless blocks of stone containing the sought-after lead and silver mix. On occasion the tunnels thinned to gaps so small the slaves would be required to squirm like snakes on their bellies to pass through, and it was said that slave children were brought into the mines to work in the particularly tight spaces and to aid in clearing the rubble as the tunnels progressed. With every blow that loosened the next group of stones came the worry that the tunnel roof might cave in, trapping the workers and leaving them perhaps to their death.[2]

The raw silver mixed with lead and stone was passed back to the surface, where it was refined and purified in vast furnaces and settling tanks. The local community had been working these mines for the best part of three millennia. But it was Hippias, son of Peisistratus, who had, while tyrant from the time of his father's death until he was forced to flee Athens in 510 BCE, first ordered the silver at Laurion to be used to create high-quality silver coinage – Athens's own coinage – stamped with an image of their patron deity Athena on one side and her favorite animal, the Little Owl, on the other. These coins had quickly become not just a powerful trading tool in a world which had only recently started regularly using coinage, but, just as important, a powerful tool in Athens's projection of its increasing power.

Silver had continued to be extracted from Laurion through the first two decades of Athens's new system of isonomia, with the mines worked on behalf of the state by elite individuals who could afford the slave army required to operate them. Nowhere was the harsh reality of the Athenians' notion of equality clearer than at Laurion: for the benefit of all equal (male) citizens of Athens, a small group of elites would make themselves even richer by working a vast slave population to death to produce a product from which they took a sizable cut, before passing the remainder on to the state.

During the early 480s, the seams of silver in the mines at Laurion had been dwindling, the slaves worked harder than ever to extract every precious ounce and follow every seam to its end. It even seemed as if the mines might finally run dry. And then in 483/2 (the year after Xanthippus was ostracized) a report came from Laurion that a new seam of silver had been discovered. It was bigger than anything seen before and as soon as it could be extracted, it promised unprecedented riches for Athens (and of course for the elites holding the leases to run the mines). In fact, the only people for whom the discovery was bad news were the ones who made it: the slaves, who now had to work even harder to quickly extract this treasure trove of silver so that Athens could put it to work. The area around Laurion became even more industrial than it had been before, with more areas to grind down the rock, lead, and silver mix; more washing areas to separate the broken rock granules from the metals; more furnaces belching smoke to heat the metal mixture to extremely high temperatures so that the metals would melt; and more distillation tanks to allow the molten metals to separate as the heavier lead fell away from the lighter silver. Southeast Attica billowed with smoke, sending a signal to all around that Athens was soon to receive a special gift from the ground.

The question was what to do with it. The natural course of action, fitting for a political system built on equality (equality at least among male citizens, since female citizens had no vote), was for the windfall to be evenly distributed as a cash handout to the entire citizen body. Herodotus estimated that this equated, in just the first year of the new seam's exploitation, to about ten drachmas per Athenian citizen (there were about thirty thousand adult male citizens).[3] This was equivalent to two weeks' wages for a skilled worker. For a low-paid worker, it was a month's wages. And who knew how many years the silver seam might continue for! The Assembly of Athenian citizens, gathered on the Pnyx to formalize the decision about what to do with the silver, could be forgiven for already dreaming about how to spend the cash. Aristides, Themistocles' long-term rival but also battle compatriot, put the case for the equal distribution of the windfall and no doubt was cheered by the vast majority of lower-income Athenian citizens.

According to Plutarch, Themistocles was the only one to stand up in the Assembly and offer a different proposition. Themistocles argued that instead of distributing the money among them all, they should collectively decide to use it to the city's benefit as a whole. The benefit would come not through the construction of another temple or building to beautify the city. Instead, it would come through the construction of something that could defend the city: a fleet. Herodotus and Plutarch agree that Themistocles was open with the political Assembly about what the money should be used for. The author of the *Constitution of the Athenians* text, on the other hand, suggested that Themistocles did not openly argue that the money should be used to build a fleet, but proposed instead that it should be given equally to the hundred richest Athenians, who would be entrusted to invest it in the smartest way possible and that Athens would then benefit from the return. If they invested poorly, Athens could require them to repay the original "loan." The author goes on to say that once this had been agreed, Themistocles then persuaded the hundred richest Athenians to each use his share to build a warship.[4]

It seems odd that Themistocles, no natural friend of Athens's elite (and often portrayed as having spent much of the 480s systematically planning ostracisms against them), would now suggest a plan to give the money to the city's wealthiest and then be assured of his ability to persuade them to do what he wanted with it. And in the heady atmosphere of the 480s, in which the city was ostracizing people at a rate unparalleled through the rest of the fifth century BCE, it does not sound like the sort of argument that would win the popular vote against an equal distribution of the money among all the citizens.

But that does not mean that Themistocles' direct argument in favor of building a fleet to defend the city found favor, either. Plutarch and Herodotus are very clear that Themistocles did not claim that this fleet was needed to defend Athens against a renewed threat from Persia. No mention appears to have been made of the fact that the Persian King Darius, defeated at Marathon in 490, had been preparing for another invasion of Greece in the early 480s, before being diverted by rebellions in Egypt and Babylonia. Darius had died in 486, and his son Xerxes had ascended the throne, beginning his reign in lightning style by quashing the rebellion in Egypt (and another in Babylon in 484) and making new preparations for an invasion of Greece. In 483 these preparations were in full swing—not just within Asia, but within northern Greece itself. In order to avoid the potential destruction of his fleet, as had happened to the expedition in 490 when violent storms had arisen in the northern Aegean, Xerxes ordered a canal to be dug through what is today's Mount Athos peninsula in Chalcidice so that his fleet could sail closer to the land and avoid the storms and rougher seas around the tip of the peninsula. Herodotus noted that this canal, 1¼ miles in length and wrought through the solid earth, was also meant to demonstrate Xerxes' power and might to the world.[5]

Yet while the construction of this canal and apparent mass moving of provisions to station points along the route Xerxes' army intended to make were taking place, as well as an initial attempt to create a pontoon bridge across the Hellespont between Asia and Greece so that Persian troops could literally march into Greece, the threat from Persia, according to Plutarch and Herodotus, was not what Themistocles chose to focus on when arguing for building a fleet. Indeed, Plutarch tells us that the mass of the Athenian people in 483/2 felt that the Persians were "a long way off and did not inspire any very serious fear that they were about to arrive."[6]

Instead, Themistocles focused on a much closer and much older Athenian rival: Aegina. Aegina was within sight of the Athenian coast, had traditionally been a stronger sea power than Athens, and had taunted and punished Athens with its mastery of the sea for decades. It was the threat of Aegina that had motivated discussions when Themistocles was archon in 494/3 – perhaps even led by Themistocles – about investing in a bigger and more defensible port at Piraeus to replace Athens's small harbor at Phaleron. Building had been going on ever since, but so had Aeginetan superiority at sea. Herodotus included an account of the Athenians' official ship of state being captured by the Aeginetans as well as numerous other ships; vital Athenian maritime trade was taken from them, and most important, of course, Athens suffered a constant loss of face.[7]

What Themistocles offered was therefore a vision of an Athens with a fleet that promised both immediate and future gains to the demos. Immediate, in that building a hundred warships would provide work and livelihoods for many Athenians (as would their upkeep in the new, enlarged port of Piraeus). And future, because that size fleet would put Aegina in its place once and for all and allow Athens to rule the seas and direct as much maritime trade as it wanted. Most important perhaps, the new fleet would allow the Athenians to find an outlet and balm for their "resentment against and jealousy of," as Plutarch put it, the Aeginetans – and what price could be put on that?[8]

It seems that Themistocles had learned the lessons of Athenian politics well – and especially those on how to craft an argument to win the approval of the people. His plan gave them an immediate payoff in terms of work to counteract the immediate payoff they were turning down in not voting to give every citizen an equal share of the Laurion money, but crucially it also showed how that immediate gain would produce further gains – particularly in improving the power and reputation of Athens. It was a masterclass in the sophia (wisdom) – the mixing of natural intelligence with political dexterity – that he had long been studying.

The investment in warships was not just a choice to provide the city with a fleet but also the beginning of a change in the nature of naval warfare. Typically, battles at sea had involved ships under both oar and sail, with groups of soldiers on board. Battle tactics included sailing along or through the enemy's line, turning, and coming alongside an enemy ship, thus allowing the soldiers to board and kill or capture the enemy soldiers and sailors and claim the ship. Ships had hitherto been praised for their lightness and swiftness of movement, which allowed them to turn and come alongside enemy vessels. The majority of the Greek fleets at the time were composed of this kind of ship.

But the Athenians now planned to invest their silver windfall in building a hundred triremes, warships of a relatively new design. These were much wider and heavier than the standard ships, with shallow drafts and low points of gravity. Their turning ability – as with their speed – did not come from their lightness but instead relied on the trireme's three levels of oars (hence the name "trireme" meaning literally "three rower"). The older design of ships had two rows of oars. The design change meant each trireme had 170 oars propelling it and could thus achieve significant speeds quickly while maintaining maneuverability. At the same time its weight meant that the ship itself, rather than soldiers aboard it, could inflict damage on enemy ships by ramming them. To this end, the front of every trireme was given a bronze-covered ramhead to inflict enough damage on the enemy vessel that it would be rendered useless. Having rammed an enemy, a trireme would be pulled away by its 170 oars and head off in search of its next prey, leaving its recent victim to sink.

Triremes were not built to journey long distances – not least because they lacked the space to carry provisions for the 170 oarsmen that would sustain them through many days at sea. They were intended for deployment on daylong journeys, often being hauled out of the water at night so the hulls could dry on the beach and not become waterlogged (which would make the ships heavier and thus less maneuverable).

Building a hundred of these triremes was an expensive business. The city – thanks to the Laurion silver – could afford it. But running these vessels and maintaining them also required a substantial outlay – one that the Athenians could not afford on the basis of the Laurion silver alone. The costs of manning, fitting out, and maintaining the ships was quickly established as an "honor" awarded to the richest men in Athenian society. These men would become the ships' captains (trierarchs) and be responsible for the ships' upkeep for a year. This honor was known as a trierarchy, and it was a heavy financial burden, equivalent to a tax on the wealthiest men in Athenian society.

The trireme quickly become a strong symbol of the developing system of people power at Athens. On one hand this was because citizens of all classes sat together rowing the ships: a citizen did not have to be wealthy enough to afford armor or horses in order to contribute to the defense of his city. And at the same time, the system of trierarchy ensured that the wealthiest citizens gave back to society by making the maintenance of a large fleet affordable for the city of Athens. Triremes thus empowered everyone to defend the city and harnessed the wealth of the elites in the service of the city.

While Themistocles seems to have persuaded the Athenians to invest in this new kind of fleet to defend Athens from the ongoing threat posed by Aegina, Plutarch argues that he also understood only too clearly the coming threat from Persia. While the rest of the Athenians might have thought that Marathon was the end of the matter, Themistocles regarded it as "merely the prelude to greater contests," for which he "kept himself oiled as an athlete." This is the centerpiece of later portraits of Themistocles as a visionary—the one person who foresaw the future in time to prepare Athens and Greece to meet it. Of course it is impossible to know whether Themistocles really had that clarity of foresight. But such foresight is certainly not a prerequisite to understand Themistocles' position on the disposition of the Laurion silver. After all, he had long been a supporter of naval power, and Aegina was stifling Athens's chances to flourish. The Laurion silver offered a once-in-a-lifetime opportunity to leap ahead of Aegina by at last building a thoroughly up-to-date fleet of triremes that would revolutionize the way battles at sea were fought. And arguing for it allowed Themistocles also to pick a quarrel with his long-term rival, Aristides, who was arguing for the money to be allocated equally across the citizen body. Perhaps Themistocles himself was, like other Athenians, wrapped up in the needs of the present and did not himself realize until several years later what a fortunate call he had made. As Herodotus put it, "Even though the ships were never used for the reason for which they had been originally built, they were at hand for Greece in her hour of need."[9]

Themistocles had now been a known figure in Athenian politics for a full decade, since service as archon in 494/3. At age forty-two, with significant political and military experience, he was entering his epoch at the epicenter of Athenian decision making, and his successful call to the people to back the building of a new fleet had given him new impetus. The ancient sources, particularly Plutarch, argue that this new energy—aside from the project of building a hundred new triremes—was directed at tipping Athens's political system further in his favor. Ostracism, which until that time might have seemed an unpredictable tool that could be used against anyone – seems to have become Themistocles' weapon of choice.

In 482, another ostracism vote was held, and this time the person chosen for ostracism was Aristides. It is hard to comprehend how a figure so renowned for justice could have ended up being singled out as someone the Athenians wished to remove from their sight. True, he had been leading the failed proposal to distribute the silver windfall equally among the citizens of Athens, and after the people decided on another use for it, he may have been seen as an impediment, especially if he continued to advocate for his own proposal. But the ancient sources also clearly point the finger at Themistocles for whipping up resentment against him. According to Plutarch's biography of Aristides, it was Themistocles who stoked the Athenians' resentment of this leading figure by claiming that he had done away with the public courts of justice, instead hearing legal disputes himself in private without any oversight and thus acting in all ways like a king. Plutarch explains that the people of Athens by this time had become extremely fond of their sense of people power and intensely disliked anyone who seemed to "tower above them." For that reason, they voted to ostracize Aristides because of their "dislike of his reputation" but gave it the public face of "fear of tyranny."[10]

The surviving ostraca from the vote against Aristides show how varied people's perceptions were of what Aristides had done to deserve his ostracism. One shard accuses him of some sort of religious offense against suppliants seeking protection. Another labels him "Datis's brother" (Datis was one of the Persian admirals who attacked Greece in 490). But perhaps the most revealing – if probably fictional – story is contained in Plutarch's Life of Aristides, in which he recounts that an illiterate country citizen of Athens approached Aristides on the day of the vote, not knowing who he was, to ask for his help in writing on a piece of pottery with which he intended to cast his vote. On being asked to write the name Aristides, Aristides asked the man what wrong Aristides had done him. "None," replied the man, "I don't even know him. I'm just fed up with hearing him everywhere called 'The Just.' " Aristides did not quibble but wrote his own name on the pottery shard. Aristides went into exile, leaving Athens in a fervor of trireme construction. Herodotus quotes the number of triremes constructed as two hundred rather than the one hundred cited by Plutarch, and the suggestion has been made that, following Aristides' departure, the assembly, perhaps encouraged by Themistocles, doubled the number.[11]

This moment may have been a tipping point for Themistocles as a political operator in Athens – the point at which he emerged from his period of learning into a period in which he was actively choosing to affect events to the utmost of his ability. From crafting and securing support for his plan for the Laurion silver to his rumored involvement in propelling Aristides toward ostracism – here is a Themistocles who was trying not simply to navigate events but to direct them. A man assured that he knew the game well enough to play it for real.

In the autumn of 481, as Athens was without doubt wholly focused on building and equipping its new triremes, as well as training its citizens as oarsmen who could work seamlessly together to power the vessels in battle, the army and fleet of the Persian King, Xerxes, gathered in western Asia Minor. At the same time, Xerxes sent a request for earth and water as tokens of submission to all the Greek city-states except Athens and Sparta. Not only had these two city-states brutally responded to his messengers previously, but also he was giving them no option of peaceful surrender. That autumn representatives of a number of Greek city-states, including Athens, met at the panhellenic shrine of Poseidon at Corinth to decide on a response. This was no grand pan-Greek alliance – approximately a tenth of all Aegean Greek cities turned up, with the majority remaining neutral or choosing to align with Persia. But those who came agreed that they would put aside their present differences (even the long-running rivalry between Athens and Aegina) and work together to repel the invasion they knew was coming. Their first step was to send out representatives to city-states they wanted to join their alliance who had not come to the initial meeting – both those geographically and thus tactically central to the defense of Greece (such as Argos) and those who, while farther away, had significant resources available, such as the tyrant Gelon of Syracuse in Sicily. At the same time, they also sent spies to Asia Minor to get a better sense of the Persian King's forces.

We are told by Herodotus that the Greek spies were discovered by Xerxes' soldiers. But instead of being killed, they were given a full tour of the troops and fleet and then sent back to Greece in order to pass on their account and cause maximum fear and confusion. The numbers of Persian troops and ships are often disputed in the sources, but without doubt, they were large – terrifyingly large. And news from many of the places to which the Greeks had sent representatives was no better: little further help was forthcoming.[12]

The beginning of 480 was a dark time for Greece, and especially Athens. Meeting after meeting of the Boule and of the full citizen body in the Assembly on the Pnyx was no doubt spent in discussion about how to proceed. Matters were not helped by consultations of the oracle at Delphi, whose Pythian priestess had initially responded to the Athenian ambassadors by declaiming, "Why are you sitting there, you fools? Leave, flee to the ends of the Earth!" The ambassadors were on the point of leaving in despair when they were encouraged by a local Delphian to offer supplication to the god and try again. This they did, receiving a less despairing but perhaps even more confusing response – one that has become famous. For the Pythian priestess is said to have claimed that Athens's only chance of survival rested on a "wooden wall."[13]

In Athens this milder but still confusing response from the highly respected oracle at Delphi now had to be interpreted. We are told by Herodotus that some of the older citizens believed that the wooden wall in question was the old wooden wall that once had surrounded the Acropolis at the heart of the city. They advised therefore that, as they had done on previous occasions, the citizenry should barricade themselves on the Acropolis. Others in the city argued, however, that the wooden wall referred collectively to the wooden hulls of the triremes they had been building over the past two years, and that they should sail out to meet the Persians at sea.[14]

It was Themistocles, characterized by Herodotus as a man "just recently emerged into prominence" in Athens, who swung the Athenian majority behind the interpretation of the wooden wall as meaning its fleet. He did so by combining the concept of the wooden wall as the fleet with a reinterpretation of another part of the oracular response about the nearby island of Salamis, just off the coast of Attica.[15]

It is recounted in Plutarch that Themistocles now sought by any means to put himself in charge of Athenian planning. In the contest for the election of Athens's key general for the campaign to come, many stood back, terrified by the danger. But one man, Epicydes, stayed in the competition against Themistocles. Plutarch tells us that Themistocles was aware of the chance that Epicydes might win the vote owing to his skillful oratory. So he paid off Epicydes to quit the election. Themistocles, in Plutarch's characterization, was sure he alone had the tenacity to lead Athens.[16]

But he did not yet have Athens's full confidence. Plutarch underlined that Themistocles wanted Athens to send its fleet to engage Persia "as far away from Greece as possible."[17] But many opposed this idea, so he and the Athenian delegation went to the next meeting of Greeks still willing to stand their ground, in spring 480, to try to find a common plan of defense. The outcome was a decision to march north to the territory of Thessaly, where the combined Greek army might be able to stem the Persian advance into central Greece at a place called the Valley of Tempe, between the great mountains of Olympus and Ossa. Ten thousand Greek troops came together in the valley, with Themistocles himself as the commander of the Athenian contingent.

Having made all that effort to come together, however, the combined Greek land forces were in the valley for only a few days when they received word from the king of Macedon, farther to the north, who was a vassal of Persia. His report was chilling: the Greek forces had no hope of stopping the Persians at the valley not just because of the overwhelming size of the Persian forces but also because there were parallel routes the Persians could take to march into central Greece through Thessaly, routes of which Themistocles and the others were apparently not aware. Staying at Tempe could lead to the Greeks being bypassed and then surrounded. Realizing the frailty of their position, Themistocles and the other Greek leaders who had journeyed to Tempe decided to return immediately to the Isthmus in central Greece, leaving the Thessalians to their fate. The Thessalians, with little choice, promptly pledged allegiance to the Persians.

All Greece as far south as Boeotia was now at best neutral or offering allegiance to Persia; Argos in the Peloponnese was taking the same, effectively pro-Persian stance. To make matters even worse, while the Greeks were traveling to, and then back from,

Tempe, Xerxes had begun the march of his army toward Greece, in close association with a massive fleet. Such was the size of his army that Herodotus recounts that it took more than seven days and nights "without a moment's break" for them all to march across the boat bridge constructed across the Hellespont. One local living on the Greek side of the Hellespont is said to have queried why the all-powerful king of the gods, Zeus, had decided to transform himself into the figure of Xerxes – such was the scale of might and power on display commanded by the King of Kings. And that power and might was heading slowly but surely toward Athens.[18]

CHAPTER SEVEN

Facing Destruction

Through June and July 480, Xerxes' troops on land and his fleet at sea inched around the Aegean to the north and began their descent toward central Greece. Plutarch argues that it was only at this point, as so many Greek communities offered allegiance to Xerxes and as Xerxes got closer and closer to Athens, that the Athenians began to pay attention to Themistocles' advice to use their superior fleet to confront Xerxes at sea.[1] Yet the majority of Greeks still willing to fight against Xerxes had few ships and more troops, so they also wanted to make a stand on land. At the rushed council meetings of the resisting city-states, a new plan was hatched, led by Sparta, to block the Persian land advance at another, better-known, narrow pass, Thermopylae, on the northeastern coast of central Greece. At the same time the Greek fleet – mainly composed of Athenian ships – would advance up the coast to take up a station near Artemisium, a shrine to Artemis at the northern tip of the island of Euboea, which was roughly parallel with Thermopylae. Such a position allowed the Greek land army and fleet to keep in communication with each other and, they hoped, to stymie the advance of the massive Persian land army and fleet at pinch points on land and at sea, where the superior Persian numbers would not count so much in their favor.

Themistocles was sent by the Athenians as their general in command of the Athenian fleet gathering at Artemisium. He was clearly perceived as a strong and trustworthy leader by the Athenian people. Yet the rest of the Greeks were adamant that they did not want an Athenian in charge of the combined fleet; they threatened to disband unless a Spartan were put in charge. Hence Themistocles, as recounted by both Herodotus and Plutarch, willingly gave supreme command of his Athenian ships to an otherwise unknown Spartan commander, Eurybiadas. In so doing, as Plutarch particularly noted, Themistocles ensured that the Greek fleet's attempts to defeat the Persians at sea were not sunk entirely before they had even begun.[2]

By the middle of August, the troops and fleet were in position, with single advance triremes stationed farther north along the coast to keep watch for the arrival of the Persians. None of them fared well; most fell prey to the Persian advance guard, causing the Greek fleet commanders to lose their nerve and retreat farther south to the waters off Chalcis in the southern half of Euboea.

But watchers left stationed on the hilltops of Euboea finally had good news to report. The main Persian fleet, as it was mooring—eight ships deep out at sea—from a narrow beach on the tip of Magnesia just north of Euboea, was caught in the middle of a severe storm that lasted four days. Herodotus recounts that more than four hundred Persian ships were destroyed, along with countless baggage and grain-supply ships. The Athenians attributed the storm to their prayers to Boreas, the god of the North Wind, to whom they later built a shrine in Athens.

Thus emboldened by these signs of divine favor, the Greek fleet returned north from Chalcis to their original station off Artemisium, in line with the Greek land army positioned at Thermopylae. By this time the Greek and Persian land forces had been in a staring contest at Thermopylae for several days. The Persian King had banked on the fact that the Greeks would lose their nerve at the sight of his army, but the Greek soldiers, in good part bolstered by the presence of the Spartan king Leonidas and his specially raised task force of three hundred Spartans, had held their ground.[3]

On the fifth day after their arrival at Thermopylae, however, in late August 480, Xerxes began to attack the Greek troops holding the pass. On the same day, the still very large remaining Persian fleet sailed round the tip of Magnesia to harbor at Aphetae, opposite Artemisium. Fifteen Persian ships were said to have mistaken the Greeks for their own fleet and as a result easily fallen into Greek hands. But, in contrast to the stout courage being displayed by the Greeks now fighting at Thermopylae, this small win for the Greek fleet does not seem to have calmed nerves. Indeed, Herodotus and Plutarch both recount that the Spartan commander of the combined Greek fleet, Eurybiadas, wanted to leave immediately and return to the Peloponnese. The Euboeans, fearing that they were about to be abandoned as the Thessalians had been, are said to have begged Eurybiadas to stay until they could evacuate their children. Eurybiadas was unconvinced, so the Euboeans turned to Themistocles, not with persuasive words but with an attractive offer of thirty talents to keep the Greek fleet at Artemisium. Herodotus records that Themistocles gave five talents to Eurybiadas to persuade him to stay and three talents to another Corinthian commander who was keen to leave, and kept the rest for himself, having ensured that the fleet would remain at Artemisium. This was not corruption in the modern sense – it was typical Athenian business practice to accept payment in return for favors.[4]

Plutarch goes farther in underlining the means to which Themistocles resorted in order to keep the fleet together. One of his own Athenian ship commanders, Architeles, was eager to sail home – mainly, according to Plutarch, because he did not have the money to pay his sailors. Themistocles is said to have encouraged these sailors to dishonor Architeles by stealing his meal, leaving Architeles facing mutiny. Pretending to come to his aid, Themistocles then sent him a food parcel with a talent of silver hidden within it, along with an encouragement and a threat: eat up and pay your crew, or else I'll tell everyone you are receiving bribes from the Persians.[5] Accepting money from other Greeks in an alliance was acceptable, but if the money came from an enemy, then it represented a dishonorable and treacherous act of bribery.

This day had already been busy for the Greek fleet (although not of course as busy as for the land army defending the pass at Thermopylae), with money moving back and forth. But it was far from over. A Greek, Scyllias, who had been aiding the Persians, now made his way to the Greek fleet commanders to inform them that the Persians had decided to send a detachment of two hundred ships around the eastern coast of Euboea in the hope of encircling and thus trapping the Greek fleet between the two Persian fleets on the western side of Euboea.[6] The Greek commanders debated whether to flee immediately to avoid the trap or to engage the two hundred-ship detachment and thus pick off a smaller section of the Persian fleet while it was separated from the remainder. This they decided to do, but first they determined to sail out and test the remaining Persian fleet at Aphetae to get a better sense of their skill and courage.

In the late afternoon, the Greek fleet sailed to meet the Persians, and the Persians in turn were tempted out to attack them. The Greeks, on prearranged signals, formed a circle with their prows pointing outward and then simultaneously all pushed outward to attack the Persian ships surrounding them. It was a brilliant tactical maneuver that resulted, according to Herodotus, in thirty Persian ships being captured, while the Persians retreated back to Aphetae overnight.[7]

That night too the forces of nature continued to act for the Greeks. The Persian fleet at Aphetae was battered by heavy rain and winds that brought back a large amount of floating debris and bodies from its recent losses at sea. But an even greater storm blew up around the eastern coast of Euboea, taking the two hundred-ship Persian detachment by surprise and all but wiping it out. When the sun emerged the next morning, the Greeks found themselves no longer facing the danger of encirclement, while the Persians suffered further significant losses. And, indeed, the Greeks' own numbers were swelled by a further contingent of ships arriving from Athens.

That day too, on land at Thermopylae, the Greek advance guard continued to hold the Persian forces at bay, as Xerxes himself observed the impasse with no doubt increasing frustration and anger. But that evening, at the end of the second day of fighting, a local Malian man named Ephialtes betrayed the Greeks, telling Xerxes about a path over the mountains that led behind the pass at Thermopylae. The Greeks had not known about this path when they had chosen Thermopylae as the place to make their stand and halt the Persian advance. They become aware of it only after they had arrived at Thermopylae, and the Spartan king Leonidas had dispatched a thousand local Phocian troops to guard it in case the Persians found it. But his forethought was to no avail: overnight between the second and third day of fighting an elite contingent of Persians made its way, led by Ephialtes, along the path, bypassing the Phocian guards, who, too late, rushed to put on their armor.

By morning, the Persian crack troops had reached the eastern end of the pass at Thermopylae.

On the morning of the third day of fighting, the Persian fleet commanders at Aphetae, conscious of their inability to inflict real losses on the Greeks and perhaps even more conscious of what Xerxes would do to them as punishment for their ineffectiveness, were determined to engage the Greek fleet in all-out battle. The Persians sailed out and formed a crescent shape encircling the Greeks at Artemisium; the Greeks in turn sailed out to meet them. The lack of open sea meant that once again the larger Persian numbers caused more havoc than help, and at the end of the day both sides withdrew, with the Persians having suffered far more casualties than the Greeks.

The same was not true of the land battle at Thermopylae. Scouts early that morning had confirmed to the Greek advance guard that the Persians had found the path, and had not been stopped by the Phocians; the Greeks would soon be surrounded. The council of Greek leaders debated their options, and Herodotus is clear that many preferred to retreat. But Leonidas, partly because of his no-surrender ideology, partly out of his desire to maintain his own honor, and partly to give some cover to the retreating Greeks, elected to stay with his own Spartan troops. The remaining Thespians and Thebans committed to staying too. Throughout that third day, these troops, especially the Spartans and Thespians, fought with fierce courage against the Persians until they were all dead. Xerxes is said to have sought out Leonidas's corpse, and then ordered the king's head be cut off and put on a spike.

The Greek fleet off Artemisium was counting the toll of a day's battle and wondering, despite the advantages of the narrow straits and the damage they had inflicted on the Persians, how long they too could sustain the onslaught. Once again, Herodotus recounts how fragile the unity of the Greek alliance was as its leaders considered withdrawing to the Peloponnese. Themistocles again stepped into the breach, suggesting that he had a plan to encourage the Persian ships coming from Ionia and Caria – places intertwined with Greece through their ancestry and culture – to desert; if this could be achieved, they would have the necessary naval power to defeat the rest of the Persian fleet. How he intended to secure the defection, Themistocles refused to say.[8]

It was at this point, as the other commanders were falling in to support Themistocles' plan (whatever it might have been), that the messenger boat from Thermopylae arrived at Artemisium with the news of the defeat and retreat of the Greeks and the final stand of the Spartans, Thespians, and Thebans. It became clear that the fleet was trying to hold a line that was now immaterial: the only option was to retreat. The battles of Thermopylae and Artemisium were over.

The heroic endeavors, particularly of the Spartans, at Thermopylae rightly dominate ancient – and, indeed, modern – accounts of this stage of the Persian invasion. The Greek fleet, in contrast, while it did ensure its own continued survival, and deliver unexpectedly heavy losses to the enemy, did not need to sacrifice itself in a final showdown. Nor, given the difficulties Themistocles is said to have confronted throughout that time in keeping the Greek fleet together, would it perhaps have been able and willing to make such a sacrifice. But what Plutarch underlines, picking up on the ancient praise poet Pindar, is that the experiences at Artemisium gave the Greeks an important insight: in the right kind of narrow straits, all the masses of showy ships in the world could not guarantee a victory against a navy committed to fighting at close quarters. Pindar called it the "planting" of the "gleaming corner-stone of liberty." Plutarch called it confidence. Both, however, were writing with the benefit of hindsight: at the time, it was far from certain whether the insight gained would be, or could be, put to good use in the near future.[9]

But perhaps we should also see these events as an important step in the development in Themistocles' way of behaving. Having moved clearly from observer and navigator of Athenian politics to proactive manipulator, here we see him in a war setting consistently managing events to achieve the ends he desired and thought best, particularly in terms of how he sought to control the behavior of others. In politics, he had sought to manage his own reputation and advancement—and, on occasion, to denigrate the reputation and hinder the advancement of others. But in this war setting, in which his only hope of survival and victory came from ensuring that others stuck with the plan and did not decide to prioritize their own survival, his actions were aimed at maintaining the unity of the Greeks, in any way possible. Perhaps Artemisium was the planting of the gleaming cornerstone of liberty in terms of understanding the tactics that could lead to victory against the superior Persian forces. But it was also the planting of a modus operandi for Themistocles: maintaining unity, and securing survival, required ever more ingenious and high-stakes maneuvers.

Around September 1, 480, the Greek fleet sailed south again from Artemisium back around the coast of Attica toward Salamis and the Isthmus. The Athenian ships, led by Themistocles, brought up the rear of the retreat. But both Herodotus and Plutarch insist that Themistocles did not completely abandon his plan to try to drive a wedge between the Persian King and his Ionian and Carian contingents. At every watering place along the coast, Themistocles sent men to leave messages for the Ionians carved into the rocks, encouraging them to desert the Persians and come over to the Greeks, or at least remain neutral (or, as Plutarch suggests, to act as the traitor within and sabotage the Persian fleet). The messages pointed to the Ionians' and Carians' shared ancestry with the Athenians and reminded them of their role in bringing mainland Greece into conflict with Persia during the Ionian Revolt nearly two decades earlier. Plutarch and Herodotus underline the two potential positive outcomes of Themistocles' action: first some Ionians and Carians might desert to the Greeks, and, second, Xerxes, on hearing of these messages, might come to doubt the Ionian and Carian contingents and thus might not wish to use them in battle in case they betrayed him.[10] Just as Themistocles seems to have embraced every technique to maintain unity on his own side, so too had he realized the power of seeking to undermine it among his opponents.

But small gestures could go only so far. As Themistocles arrived back with his fleet at Attica, two things became clear. First, the Persians were now on the move south, by land and sea, conquering everything in their path. Second, the majority of the Greek army and fleet had no further desire to try to stop the Persian invasion north of the Isthmus. This stretch of land, eight miles across at its widest point and less then four at its narrowest, connected the Peloponnese to the rest of mainland Greece, and was now judged to be the best location in which to halt the Persian advance. The full weight of the collective Greek army was already starting to build a massive defensive wall across the Isthmus from one coast to the other. Athens and Attica stood north of the defensive wall and the Isthmus, and it began to dawn on the Athenians that the other Greeks were not likely to come to help save Athens from the Persian advance.

In those heady days of early September 480, the Athenians collectively decided to do something unprecedented – evacuate and abandon their city. Children, the elderly, and portable possessions were to be sent to Troezen, Salamis, or Aegina (by now on the same side as the resisting Greeks), and every able-bodied man was to ready himself for combat. This was a city-wide evacuation, and it was accomplished within days. Approximately thirty thousand male citizens, and a total population, including women, children, the elderly, and slaves, of well over a hundred thousand had to move with what they could carry themselves or that could be loaded on pack animals and carts, leaving behind the rest of their possessions. All were seeking to escape Athens through the same narrow, bumpy, uneven roads. All pushing and shoving to board the boats to their escape destinations. And they had to say goodbye to the men who were to join the ships to fight, enduring the exhaustion and terror of not knowing whether there would be enough time to get to safety, or whether they would ever see loved ones again.

Herodotus notes that despite the vast scope of the undertaking, there was relatively little delay, something he attributes to the Athenians' wish to comply with the earlier oracular pronouncement about a wooden wall being their savior – a wooden wall that Themistocles had encouraged them to understand as their fleet. But he also underlines another important portent that emerged at that moment. It had long been believed that a sacred serpent lived on the Acropolis; this serpent was fed once a month with an offering of a honey cake. The honey cake always disappeared – presumed to have been eaten – but on this occasion it remained untouched, prompting the Athenians to believe that the serpent, and perhaps thus the goddess herself, had deserted the Acropolis, as they themselves should.

Herodotus is careful not to attribute the signaling of the portents and the plans for evacuation directly to Themistocles – he saw these as collective decisions of the Athenians. But Plutarch puts Themistocles center stage. It was Themistocles who, realizing how little time was left, abandoned rational arguments and relied instead on the power of divine portents to inspire action, "like a playwright deploying machinery in a tragedy." It was Themistocles who "supplied the story" of what the untouched honey cake meant—the abandonment of the city by the goddess. It was Themistocles who reminded the Athenians of the Delphic oracular pronouncement and the understanding of its "wooden wall" as their ships. And it was Themistocles who proposed a formal decree that the city should be abandoned, the men of military age should embark on the triremes, and children, wives, and slaves should be sent to safety, as well as proposing that Athenians who had been exiled or ostracized (including his old rival Aristides) should be allowed to return and fight for Athens. Plutarch even goes so far as to recount an earlier source that claims that Themistocles was responsible for finding a large cache of hidden money with which to pay for the manning of the triremes, rather than using the funds allocated by the Council of the Areopagus. In Plutarch, we see an image of Themistocles as the active manipulator par excellence of the Athenian people.[11]

We cannot be sure of the role Themistocles played in inciting the people of Athens to make their momentous decision. But what is clear is that over time, as people looked back on this moment in Athens's history, they increasingly desired to see Themistocles as the central motivator of it.

In 1960, an inscription was published that had been found in a field near Troezen in the Peloponnese. It was a decree of the "Boule and the People" of Athens, proposed by Themistocles. The text of the decree outlines the decision of the Athenians to abandon their city to the gods and to evacuate their women and children to Troezen and their elderly and their property to Salamis. It then stipulates in great detail that all men of military age should be organized to man the two hundred Athenian triremes, in order to "resist the barbarian for the sake of their liberty and that of the other Greeks." It is a document filled with the tension of the moment: the decree records that the manning of the triremes should "start tomorrow," and also covers the recall of those ostracized and those who had hitherto been deprived of their citizen rights.[12]

On the face of it, this seems like proof that Themistocles was at the center of these monumental decisions made by the Athenians. But the decree has been subject to a huge amount of scholarly discussion because it contains several inconsistencies. First, the opening formula of the decree is one that, while it would become the standard formula used by the Athenian democracy during the later fifth and fourth centuries BCE, was not the standard in the first two decades of the fifth century. Second, some scholars argue that analysis of the letter forms of the inscription show that this copy of the decree probably dates from nearer 300 BCE than 480. And finally, the surviving inscribed text suggests that once the fleet was manned, half would be sent to support fighters at Artemisium. If so, the text would be at odds with the narrative in Herodotus and Plutarch that the decision to abandon the city was taken only after the defeat at Thermopylae and the fleet's return from Artemisium.

What we are looking at therefore, most likely, is a decree that was produced around 300 BCE, 180 years after the event, and set up at Troezen in the Peloponnese as part of the ongoing commemoration of what had come to be a historic moment in Athens's history. Not only would this theory account for the letter forms and the employment of what was by then a formulaic introduction, but it could also explain how a number of different moments and decisions had been conflated into a single decree, and also why Themistocles is put at the heart of it—because that was how, by that time, the Greeks wanted to remember events. It is therefore a helpful testament not only to the Athenians' perception of the importance of that moment in their history but to the growing view of Themistocles as an Athenian hero, particularly gifted for his foresight and vision.

Yet even if we accept this later picture of Themistocles as being central to Athenian decision making in these crucial days, we also need to be realistic about his ability to single-handedly call the shots. Writers like Plutarch, while ascribing the plans for the Athenians' next steps to Themistocles, also make it clear that Themistocles' calls to action would have fallen flat if other well-respected elite members of Athens had not also thrown their weight behind them. Chief among these was Cimon, who was said to have personally shown himself willing to evacuate the city in support of Themistocles' proposal. Rather than imagining an Athens in which the people simply followed Themistocles' directives, we must see a situation in which Themistocles, while potentially the person who suggested the next steps, was powerless to make them happen without the wider support of the elite Athenians from whom the people took their cues. This was perhaps the next step in Themistocles' political education: even the strongest leader needs other strong supporting voices on occasion.

Herodotus tells us that the fleet which had returned from Artemisium had docked at Salamis, whereas the rest of the Greek allied fleet was waiting at Troezen farther south in the Peloponnese. The Troezen fleet now moved up to join the ships at Salamis, and the united force was once again put under the control of the Spartan Eurybiadas. Eurybiadas brought the commanders of the different contingents together for a council of war and asked them all to nominate the place they thought best suited for a battle against the Persian fleet. The overwhelming majority voted to retreat back to the Isthmus, in line with the Greek land army, to pitch battle with the Persian fleet in the waters of the Peloponnese.

The evacuation of Athens had happened just in time. Within days of the Athenians taking to the ships and, according to Herodotus, while this latest council of war was itself being held, news came that the Persians, having conquered their way through Phocis and Boeotia, torching the cities of Thespiae and Plataea, which had refused to surrender to the Persian King, were now in the territory of Athens.[13]

From their ships off Salamis, the Greeks could only watch as smoke cloud after smoke cloud began to rise, charting the course of the Persians' devastation of Attica. Soon the Persians were in the heart of the deserted city of Athens itself, stripping it bare and setting it on fire. The Athenians on board the ships were probably close enough not only to see the smoke clouds but, as the winds turned in their direction, to smell the burning of their city and perhaps even to hear the unstoppable passage of flame destroying structure after structure, as well as the no doubt joyful and celebratory cries of the masses of Persians flooding the city, looting whatever the Athenians had left behind. Perhaps too even those who had been evacuated to Salamis, Aegina, and Troezen could see the smoke clouds rising in the distance, symbolizing the loss of everything they had built through their lives. The Persians had now taken from the Athenians their own home: no doubt now that every Athenian heart beat with merciless hatred for the Persian enemy.

The only place that held out was the Acropolis. It was, of course, a natural defensive position – it had been the place to which supporters of Hippias the tyrant had retreated in the days of Themistocles' youth to try to hold out against the Spartans. It was the place where too the supporters of Cleisthenes' opponent Isagoras had retreated when besieged by the mass of the Athenian people bent on bringing about political change and enacting Cleisthenes' proposals. Here the final remnant of the Athenian population that had decided to remain in Athens – those who had not agreed with the interpretation of the "wooden wall" as meaning Athens's ships and believed it instead to be the old wooden wall of the Acropolis, along with some of the faithful temple servants who had vowed to serve their deities to the end – stood, waiting for the Persian attack. They had defended themselves as best as they were able, barricading the entrance points with doors, planks, and whatever else they could find. They looked down to see not the beautiful buildings of their famous city but a swirling swarm of Persians on all sides, devouring everything in their path, and gathering to attack.[14]

Ironically, the Persians, we are told, saw the wooden barricades thrown up against them as the weakest point of the Acropolis's defenses. They took up position on the Areopagus – once the seat of the highest council in Athens, where Themistocles and others had debated the significant issues of the day – wrapped cloth around their arrow heads, and set them alight, firing at the wooden barricades. But even as their walls were consumed by the flames, the defenders of the Acropolis would not give in, rolling boulders down the slopes to prevent the enemy's advance. The Persians sent descendants of the now nonagenarian Athenian tyrant Hippias, whom they had brought with them, to try to talk sense into the defenders and persuade them to surrender. They failed. Despite their enormous manpower, the Persians were, for a brief time, stumped, just as they had been temporarily at Thermopylae.

Sometime around September 23, 480, the Persians, as they had at Thermopylae, found a way around the courageous defenders. They sent a small detachment to scale the sheerest side of the Acropolis, which had been left undefended, as it was thought impossible to breach. When these soldiers reached the summit, they moved immediately to open the main gates and allow in the bulk of the enemy. Herodotus tells us that some of the Athenian defenders, seeing the Persians on the summit, threw themselves from the Acropolis to their deaths. Others crowded as suppliants into the main temple of Athena, hoping that the Persians would not attack them in this place of safety. According to Herodotus, the Persians killed every last one, looted the sanctuary, and set the Acropolis on fire.[15]

It was this final grand column of acrid dark smoke rising from the great Acropolis at the heart of Athens that signaled the fall of the city.[16] And the commanders of the different contingents of Greek ships coming from twenty-two Greek cities, all harbored at Salamis, took from it a very clear message: they must retreat back to the Isthmus, to make a stand at sea buttressed by their armies on land.

Themistocles returned to his ship that night with the lamentable news that the Greeks were intending to head for the Isthmus. He was met by Mnesiphilus, the man to whom Plutarch believes Themistocles had long attached himself as his adviser and guide, and with whom he had probably negotiated the turbulent politics of Athens during the 480s. Herodotus suggests that it was Mnesiphilus who now advised Themistocles to take a strong stand against the commanders' decision. His reasoning was simple: if the Greek fleet were to withdraw any farther, then the alliance would disintegrate, and every Greek would fight only for his own city, rather than for Greece as a whole. The Greeks would stand no chance against the Persians, who would pick them off one by one.

Themistocles, Herodotus recounts, immediately left to speak with the overall commander of the Greek fleet, Eurybiadas, laying out Mnesiphilus's arguments as his own. Eurybiadas, often portrayed in the sources as a leader without great conviction or inspirational leadership of his own, was persuaded to call the leaders of the Greek contingents back together again.

This next meeting of the Greek commanders is notorious—recounted in detail in both Herodotus and Plutarch. Even though Eurybiadas was in overall command, Themistocles apparently did not wait for him to open the meeting, but jumped in immediately to press his view that the fleet must remain at Salamis. To this another of the commanders (Herodotus has it as the Corinthian leader, Plutarch as Eurybiadas himself) retorted, "In the games, those who are too quick off the mark are given a beating." To which Themistocles replied, "Yes, but those who get left behind do not win the victory crown."[17]

These remarks set the tone for the meeting. Themistocles, not wanting to make the argument to the generals themselves that they would forget the alliance and defend only their own cities if the fleet retreated, instead put forward the plan to stay at Salamis as the best strategic option to ensure victory, because it enabled them to fight in the narrows, where their smaller numbers would not be overwhelmed by the larger and more maneuverable Persian fleet. This was the lesson they had learned from Artemisium and one which they needed to reapply. Moreover, he appealed to the mention of Salamis in the Delphic oracle as meaning the gods demanded that it be the place where the Greeks stopped the Persian advance.

But Themistocles' logic was not enough to turn the room. The Corinthian commander accused him of being a man without a city—since Athens had been abandoned—and thus not worthy of being listened to or empowered to bring a motion to the council. To which Themistocles replied with the brutal truth: Athens might be in ruins and its people scattered, but the men of Athens were crewing 180 war triremes. This was the biggest contingent by far within the Greek fleet, dwarfing the next biggest, the Corinthians, who had 50 ships, Aegina after that with 30 ships, and the Spartans with only 16 ships. (The other commanders had even fewer.) In total the Greeks probably had 368 ships, so the Athenian triremes composed almost 50 percent of the Greek fleet. If the Athenians were to decide to turn their backs on the Greeks, Themistocles intimated, the rest of the Greeks would be lost.[18]

Themistocles repeated his threat again to Eurybiadas: stay at Salamis or the Athenian fleet, and the Athenian people, will leave and set up a new Athens in Italy, leaving the rest of Greece to its fate. Themistocles, seemingly, had left the Greeks with no choice: they would stay and fight at Salamis. It was not the first time Themistocles had taken away choices in order to ensure a unity of purpose. But it was perhaps the first time that he had sought to do so on such a large scale, speaking on behalf of the entire Athenian fleet in order to influence the rest of the Greeks. The stakes – for Themistocles, for the Athenians, and for the Greeks – could not have been higher.

CHAPTER EIGHT

The Hero Rises—And Falls

The earthquake came at dawn on September 24, 480. The Greeks responded with prayers to their gods but also with a call to arms: not to their men, who already lay waiting on land and in their ships, but to the demi-gods and heroes who might help them in the forthcoming conflict. The heroes they chose were local: Ajax and his father, Telamon, who were said to reside on and look after the island of Salamis, and Telamon's father, Aeacus, who resided on Aegina and was also the grandfather of Achilles. But Aeacus was too far away to help them with the battle at Salamis. A ship was duly dispatched to Aegina with an empty couch on the deck to "pick up" the mythical hero and give him somewhere comfortable to sit while journeying to join his son and grandson, Telamon and Ajax, on Salamis.

The earthquake was not the first sign from the gods. The night before, according to Plutarch, as Themistocles was threatening Athenian withdrawal if the Greek fleet did not stay at Salamis, an owl was observed to perch on the masthead of the ship where Themistocles was speaking. The goddess Athena, it appeared, was supporting Themistocles' plan.[1]

But all the gods and heroes in the world could not steady the nerves of the Greek naval commanders when they started to see the Persian fleet draw up in lines against them. The ships came all day, more and more, as their king, Xerxes, took up position on the hilltops above the Straits of Salamis, so he could personally bear witness to their valor and victory. The Persian fleet was so big, despite the destruction wrought on it by storms and battles around Artemisium and Euboea, that it took the entire day to assemble. Night was already falling by the time the last ships had arrived. Battle would need to wait for the next day, and the two sides would have to spend an uneasy night contemplating their fates.

It was a night which once again broke the resolve of the Greek commanders. Those with homes in the Peloponnese longed to sail for the Isthmus. No amount of war council discussion, or interpretation of divine portents, or even threats that the Athenians would leave the rest of the Greeks to their fate could persuade them otherwise, and they began to pass down the orders to set sail before dawn came.

At this moment, when arguments and threats could no longer overcome the fear of the Greek commanders, Themistocles once again took matters into his own hands. Determined to ensure that the Greeks had no choice but to stand and fight, he turned to the slave tutor of his children, a man called Sicinnus, and ordered him to deliver a message to the Persian King. That message, as we saw at the start of this book, was framed as a betrayal of the Greeks. Themistocles offered to join the Great King's side and as a token of his allegiance relayed crucial information: the Greeks were trying to slip away. The King, he warned, must not allow them to escape but must attack and destroy their fleet immediately, while they were in disarray and disagreement and as likely to fight among themselves as against the Persians.[2]

Xerxes believed Themistocles' message. It was, after all, nearly true: the Greeks *were* in disarray and disagreement, and many were intending to flee. But was it true that Themistocles now sought to join the King's side – or at least sought to lay the groundwork for such a move if the Greeks were defeated? Or was this the necessary subterfuge that would ensure that the key message – the need to prevent the Greeks from slipping away during the night by attacking them while they were hidden in the narrow Straits of Salamis – was believed? Was it the work of Themistocles the traitor, intent on his own personal survival? Or Themistocles the ultimate manipulator of people, of armies, and now of the King of Kings?

The stakes were enormous. If Themistocles' message were discovered by the Greeks, he would have been condemned immediately as a traitor. Themistocles was putting his life on the line to ensure that a battle took place. And while it is impossible to completely rule out that he may also have been seeking to ensure the goodwill of the Persian King toward him if the Greeks were defeated, it seems much more likely that his course of action was motivated by the deeply held belief that it was the right thing for the Greeks, bolstered by the confidence to take such a risk. His confidence was not just born out of the experience of fighting within a disciplined cohesive whole at Marathon or seeing the tactical advantage of taking on a superior navy in the narrow straits at Artemisium. It was also fueled by more than twenty years in Athenian politics, during which Themistocles had become comfortable with a succeed-big-or-fail-big mentality; with standing alone to promote a particular course of action; with moving from navigator of the balancing act to becoming a manipulator of it; with going to any lengths when convinced of the necessity of a course of action, both in politics and in war. His twenty-year education in practical politics had nurtured in Themistocles the confidence to attempt the ultimate manipulation: of rulers, of armies, and of the course of history.

During the night the Persian fleet was given orders to sail out from Phaleron Bay and fan out in an arc around Salamis to cut off the escape route for the Greek fleet. Midway through the night, the Greeks had become trapped, although they were unaware of it—they were still arguing among themselves. It was at that moment that the long-term great rival of Themistocles, Aristides, arrived by ship from Aegina. He called Themistocles out of the war council and told him that not only must they now put aside their rivalry and fight together for the good of Athens (as some sources claim they had also agreed to do when fighting together at Marathon) but that the Greeks were now surrounded. Themistocles apparently could not have been more delighted to know that Sicinnus's message had got through. According to Herodotus, he even told Aristides that he had sent word to the Persians to encourage it. Herodotus does not tell us how Aristides reacted to this news, but Plutarch suggests that he saw the wisdom in putting the Greeks in a bind and praised Themistocles for his actions.[3]

It seems also that Themistocles remembered the lesson of the evacuation of Athens: sometimes even the strongest leaders need the support of other strong voices to win their point. The two agreed that the Greek council of war needed to hear the news of the Persian advance from a separate trusted source: Aristides. But even after they learned about the movement of the Persian fleet from this most trustworthy man, the war council remained unconvinced. It took the arrival later that night of a ship from Tinos, a Greek Cycladic Island community that had initially sided with the Persians but had now changed allegiance, bearing the same news, to convince the council that the Greeks were really surrounded.

As dawn broke, and the first rays of sunlight allowed the Greeks to catch glimpses of the Persian ships fanned out from Phaleron to Salamis, the commanders finally realized they had no choice but to fight. Themistocles is said by Herodotus to have embraced the opportunity, giving a rallying speech and asking every man to focus on the best aspects of human nature and fight to preserve them. His speech was buoyed by the arrival of the ship from Aegina "carrying" the hero Aeacus to join the Greek ranks. According to Plutarch, however, Themistocles was forced to do more than give a rousing speech. The fleet's seer – interpreter of omens – who was overseeing the pre-battle religious rite, demanded the slaughter of three Persian prisoners of war as a human sacrifice to the god Dionysus. Themistocles, having so often called on divine signs to support his actions and ideas, could not contradict the seer, especially at such a crucial time. The men of the Greek fleet – high on adrenaline, fear, and blood lust for the battle – roared for these ultimate offerings to the gods. Themistocles was for once outmaneuvered, and gave them what they wanted.[4]

Battle was joined on September 25. Plutarch suggests that by this time all the Greeks had accepted Themistocles' advice about when and how to fight, whereas Herodotus reports that each Greek commander was now committed to securing the best reputation for himself and making his own decisions.[5] Both versions could, of course, be to some extent true. What worked for the Athenians most spectacularly, in addition to the fact that the Persians were encouraged to fight in a narrow strait where they could send only one wave of ships at a time, thus nullifying their superior numbers, was that as the battle and the day progressed, the winds and waves combined to make conditions in the Straits of Salamis much choppier. Athenian triremes were built to be wide and low in the water, with shallow drafts. They were less affected by the strong winds and waves than the Persian ships, designed with high decks and sides, whose maneuverability became sluggish, often exposing them side-on to the ramming attacks the triremes had been specifically designed to deliver.

The battle lasted all day, with the Aeginetan ships in particular performing heroic feats. Themistocles commanded the Athenian fleet, while Aristides commanded the Athenian troops that landed on the small island in the middle of the Straits of Salamis that had been taken over by Persian forces during the night. He promptly put them all to slaughter. By nightfall, the Greeks had their victory. Plutarch, as we saw in the Prologue, echoed the poet Simonides in claiming it to be the most brilliant exploit ever performed at sea by Greeks or "barbarians" and attributed it to the courage and enthusiasm of all who fought in the battle, but particularly to the good judgment and cleverness of Themistocles. That the rest of the Greek commanders echoed this view – at least in a roundabout way – was shown sometime later, when they reconvened at the Isthmus after the battle in order to cast their votes for who should be declared the bravest individual in the battle. Each voted for himself first but all voted for Themistocles second. As a result, in the second round of voting, Themistocles emerged the victor. But so jealous were the other Greeks of his success that they refused to accept the vote and sailed off to their own cities without declaring anyone the bravest.[6] Perhaps some warning bells went off in Themistocles' mind, reminding him of the importance of that balancing act between strong leadership and not getting too big for one's boots that had been so vital in Athenian politics during the 480s. But given the speed and enormity of events, for him to heed such a warning would perhaps have been too much to expect, even for someone as attuned to the highs and lows of political life as Themistocles.

In the immediate aftermath of the battle, however, both sides were unsure about what would happen next. The Greek victory was significant but not a death blow to either the enormous Persian fleet or, indeed, its even more enormous and relatively untouched land army. Would the Persian fleet regroup and attack again? Would it attempt to build bridges across the Straits of Salamis to march troops onto the island? Should the Greeks go on the offensive and attack again?

Within twenty-four hours of the defeat at Salamis, however, the surviving Persian ships left Phaleron Bay in the dead of night and sailed back toward the Hellespont and the Persian bridges. They left, according to Herodotus, on the orders of the King, to protect the Persian bridges across the Hellespont. Clearly Xerxes feared that the Greeks might go on the offensive and attempt to cut him off and trap him and his army in Greece.

Discovering the flight of the Persian fleet, the Greek fleet immediately set sail in pursuit, leaving a small contingent behind to defend Salamis from the still present Persian army and Xerxes himself, who still occupied Attica (and the city of Athens). The Greeks assumed that the Persians would make straight for the Hellespont, and therefore they sailed in a similar line, coming within a day's rowing to what they thought would have been the Persians' first point of call: the island of Andros.

Andros had been conquered by the Persians in 490, when they had first sailed across the Aegean to attack Athens at Marathon. The Persians had continued to extract tax from the island, and during Xerxes' invasion had demanded that Andros contribute ships to the Persian fleet. It was, in effect, enemy territory.

The Greeks, not finding the Persian fleet at Andros to engage, now held a further council of war. Themistocles urged them to push on and pursue the Persian fleet all the way to the Hellespont so they could do exactly what Xerxes feared: trap the Persians in Greece. The Spartan commander Eurybiadas, despite Themistocles' having proved his strategic abilities in arguing in favor of engaging the Persians at Salamis rather than retreating past the Isthmus, opposed the idea of now fighting the Persians on the other side of the Aegean. He was unhappy about the idea both of sailing so far from the Isthmus when the Persian army was still in Athens and of trapping the Persian King and his forces in Greece. What the Greeks wanted, he argued, was for the Persians to leave, not to have them cornered and fighting for survival in Greece.[7]

Themistocles realized that, with the exception of his Athenian commanders, who were game to follow him to the Hellespont, the rest of the Greek fleet was in agreement with Eurybiadas. Knowing that no amount of persuasion could change the minds of the Greek commanders, and this time having no way to force their hand, he ensured that he was seen not as having been defeated in the council of war but as in agreement with the majority position. Herodotus recounts that he went on to address the full assembly of the Athenian fleet—perhaps some fifteen thousand men—to "persuade them" that it was right not to pursue the Persians.[8]

Themistocles, however, did not stop there but chose, once again, to act alone. He reportedly sent Sicinnus, his Persian slave, to deliver another message to the Persian King, this time to nudge him and his land army into retreat. Themistocles' message suggested that the Greeks did indeed intend to destroy the Persian bridges across the Hellespont, but that he, Themistocles, would delay them as long as he could to allow the Persians time to flee, such was his respect for Xerxes.

Perhaps it had already been Xerxes' plan to retreat, or perhaps Themistocles' message tipped the balance. But a week after the Battle of Salamis, and a little less since he had sent the fleet back to the Hellespont, on October 2, Xerxes himself left Attica and began to move by land back up through the Greece he had ravaged so recently.

Once the Persians arrived in Thessaly, about two hundred miles to the north, Xerxes parted company with the majority of his army and his commanders. He left the Persian general Mardonius in charge of the army and told him to prepare for a new campaign the following year. Xerxes then traveled the final three hundred miles around the northern coast of the Aegean back to the Hellespont with a small contingent of troops as his guard. They moved rapidly – fearful perhaps of attack en route but also with the warning of Greek plans given to them by Themistocles. By mid-December, Xerxes was probably at the Hellespont and within sight of the route back to home turf. But those precious bridges – which Xerxes had been made to think were at risk from the Greeks – were not usable. They had been damaged by storms. The remaining Persian fleet, which had sailed to the Hellespont immediately after Salamis, now had to ferry the Persian troops across the water.

Thus, about a week after the Battle of Salamis, Athens and Attica were safe, and the Athenians began to return to their homes from their places of evacuation on Salamis and Troezen. They returned to a city in ruins – in particular, their grand sanctuaries and their precious Acropolis. But Themistocles and his Athenian fleet did not return to Athens as soon as it was free.

Instead, Themistocles gave his Athenian fleet, anchored off Andros, something else to turn their energies against, the island of Andros itself. The Andrians had, after all, sided with the Persians (although in the cold light of day, what other option – except destruction – did they have?). As "traitors," the Andrians were confronted with two very different messages. On one hand, the Greek fleet as a whole had communicated that they were there to "liberate" the Andrians from their Persian masters. On the other,

Themistocles told them that they would henceforth need to pay tribute to the Athenian fleet: their "liberty" was to be the arrival of a new master. Themistocles told the Andrians that the money was required to pacify the two gods the Athenians had brought with them: Persuasion and Compulsion. The Andrians, according to Herodotus, replied that their two goddesses were Poverty and Helplessness and that, in the service of their gods, they would not pay anything.[9]

Themistocles then laid siege to the capital city on the island and at the same time spread word to other islands, which had similarly capitulated to Persia, of what he, in the name of the whole Greek fleet, was doing. Many, knowing something of Themistocles' reputation among the Greek commanders, believed that he could persuade the Greeks as a whole to lay siege to them, particularly given what Andros was suffering, so they paid up. Herodotus claims that as a result Themistocles raked in huge amounts of money. In doing so, he was not acting atypically; it was the custom of the time for victorious commanders to seek to benefit by inflicting their will over others.

Some islands, like Paros, paid up and managed to avoid any further conflict. But the men of Carystos on Euboea were not as fortunate. Even after they paid Themistocles, he laid siege to their territory and wasted it. This almost immediate turn toward more powerful Greek communities, such as Athens, preying on weaker ones, stands in stark contrast to the Greek unity that the veterans of Salamis apparently sought to encapsulate in their commemoration of the battle. For when the fleet returned from their pursuit of the Persians and subsequent bullying of Greek cities that had sided with the enemy, they gathered up the booty extracted from their victories and other activities, then dedicated the "first fruits" of the spoils to the gods in gratitude for their victory. With these funds, they commissioned a statue of a man, some twelve cubits (eighteen feet) in height, with a model ship in the palm of his outstretched hand, to be dedicated to the god Apollo at Delphi. It was placed on the temple terrace, facing the altar in front, at the spot where visitors to the sanctuary emerged onto the terrace.

It was an unmissable location for the declaration of the Greeks' victory. But what made their statement of worship, thanks, and celebration more interesting was the inscription on the base of the statue. Most of the blocks of that inscription survive; the only part missing is the crucial first word, which indicates who was making the dedication. Scholars have offered some educated guesses, based on how the letters in the two lines of the inscription line up. This tells us how many letters were in the word describing the dedicators. (It is also clear that the word has to be in the plural because of the ending of the verb later in the line.) Two French scholars, Didier Laroche and Anne Jacquemin, have suggested that one of the main contenders is "Hellenes," "the Greeks." While this is by no means certain (and other suggestions such as *summaxoi*, "the allies," would also work), if the Greeks did use "Hellenes" to describe themselves on this dedication in honor of their victory at Salamis, it would be not only a strong demonstration of their sense of unity and common identity in the face of the Persian threat, but the first time in a surviving formal inscription that they had described themselves as "the Greeks." While it is clear that not all Greeks by any means were present at Salamis, a sense of the Greeks as a community was potentially forged in the heat of battle there, even if that same community – or at least certain members of it (in particular Athens) – immediately chose to turn on the Greeks who had not fought.[10]

This fraught conception of Greek unity went along with an ongoing tussle for individual recognition of glory among the communities that had fought at Salamis. At Delphi, in short order after the establishment of the Salamis Apollo erected (potentially) by "the Greeks," competing monuments connected with the battle were also erected to champion the achievements of individual communities. Other communities chose to commemorate their centrality to the Salamis victory within their home cities.[11] This memorialization of the ongoing competition between Greek communities to claim a crucial role in the victory reflects the vote taken by the commanders when they met at the Isthmus following the Battle of Salamis (in which each voted for himself first and Themistocles second as the most important commander, then sailed home without awarding the prize). It was also a debate that would rumble on for decades – one in which Herodotus himself would later feel obliged to weigh in (with what was apparently an unpopular view):

> I feel obliged to express an opinion which the majority of people will find hard to accept. . . . If the Athenians had been intimidated into fleeing Greece or indeed surrendering to the Persians, then no one would have decided to fight the Persians on the sea. And if no one had fought the Persians at sea, then what would have happened on the land? . . . Greece would certainly have come under Persian rule. . . . As it is, anyone who suggests that the Athenians are the saviors of Greece is absolutely correct.[12]

Themistocles himself appears to have been eager to receive recognition not just for Athens's achievements, but also for his own. After the commanders refused to recognize him in their vote at the Isthmus, he traveled to Sparta, where the Spartans, while giving their own prize of valor to their commander Eurybiadas, also gave Themistocles a special prize in recognition of his cleverness and cunning, as well as a special escort when he left Sparta. It is unclear how much the Spartans, or indeed the wider community of Greeks who had fought at Salamis, knew at the time about what Themistocles had done to make his predictions come true by sending Sicinnus to the Persian King to entice him to encircle the Athenians and, subsequently, to encourage him to retreat. But these stories of how he tricked the Persians, circulating in the years after the battle, certainly helped cement the reputation of Themistocles as a confident master manipulator, a skill not given to him simply "by nature," but one fashioned through long experience and nurture in the bosom of Athenian politics.

This singling out of Themistocles did not go down well in Athens. On his return to the city, a man named Timodemus complained that the honors paid by Sparta to Themistocles should have been paid to Athens as a whole. Themistocles put him in his place by saying that Athens was great – but so was Themistocles. Both were essential to winning honor and glory. His point was simple: he was as much part of the winning formula as Athens was.[13] It is perhaps the first time we see an image of Themistocles not in learning mode, or indeed in successful manipulator mode, but as someone overwhelmed by his own success and, crucially, as someone who has begun to forget the first rule of Athenian politics: the city – however much a person does for it – will turn on anyone who seems to be acting more for his own benefit more than the city's.

The Athenians at this point were happy to accept Themistocles' portraying himself as the tip of the Athenian spear. They knew that his reputation had quickly spread far and wide – he was said to have been a greater draw for people attending the Olympic Games to gawp at than any of the competitors.[14] That did not mean that everyone admired him. A man from Rhodes, Timocreon, for example, wrote a song about how Themistocles had taken his money and enjoyed his hospitality and yet still betrayed him. These were harsh accusations, for they charged Themistocles with breaking the fundamental societal and religious conventions of respecting those who gave him welcome and hospitality (as well, of course, as the people one did business with). But at the time, the Athenians were content to allow some individual celebrations of Themistocles and ignore his detractors. This did not mean they intended to further enhance his personal esteem, or necessarily to continue to trust his judgment in leading them.

Athens's position was still very uncertain. The city, after all, was in ruins. Athens – and Attica – was vulnerable, both to the Persian army, which had retired to Thessaly for the winter but which was inevitably, come the fighting season of 479, going to attack again, and to attack by other Greek cities. The Athenians still had much to do to ensure their city's survival. And this time no fleet could save them. They knew that a land battle was coming.

As the campaigning season of 479 BCE began, it became clear that the Athenians had chosen to put their trust in leaders other than Themistocles. The land army of Athenian hoplites was put under the command of Themistocles' old rival, Aristides, and the navy – perhaps an even greater insult given Themistocles' prowess at sea – was put under the command of another well-known Athenian at the time, Xanthippus, who had led the prosecution of Miltiades after his failed campaign against Paros, then been ostracized by the Athenians in 484 and later recalled along with other exiles just before the Persian invasion.

Themistocles does not even seem to have been elected to the board of ten Athenian generals. He completely disappears from Herodotus's narrative of events after Salamis. In his Life of Themistocles, Plutarch is forced to gloss over the great events of 479, when Sparta, commanding Athenians alongside other Greeks, secured a land victory over the Persian army at Plataea, not far from the borders of Attica, and finally succeeded in forcing the Persian army to leave Greece for good. Themistocles seems to have had no role in leading these forces, although presumably he fought in the battles as a citizen of Athens; he was still, in his mid-forties, considered to be very much of fighting age. Nor, even more surprising, does he seem to have had any leading role in the subsequent chase by the Greek fleet across the Aegean to catch the remaining Persian ships that had beached themselves at a place called Mycale on the western coast of Asia Minor. The Greek fleet, still under the overall command of the Spartans, burned the remaining Persian boats on the beach, driving the final nail in the coffin of the Persians' defeat. But Themistocles is not mentioned once in connection with these events.

Themistocles' career at this point was enough of a roller-coaster ride to leave one's head spinning, as he moved from being at the center of events leading to breaking the back of the Persian military machine at Salamis, to being feted for his actions in Sparta and becoming renowned across Greece, to almost immediately being dropped from the decision-making team and reduced to an ordinary soldier in the ranks. Themistocles was of course no stranger to seeing individuals in Athens rise to glory and descend again just as quickly (and indeed, in his successor Xanthippus's case – rise again once more). He would have been only too familiar with this career trajectory, particularly for those who were thought to have become more interested in their own glory than that of the city. And perhaps he may even have recognized that a reputation for cleverness and manipulation, such as his, was not always the greatest asset in a society like Athens, whose population did not wish to see itself as easily manipulated. We can only imagine the impact that being cast aside had on him, he who had been so central to Athenian actions in the period 484–480, especially given how keenly we are told he had felt the dishonor when others, such as Miltiades, got so much more glory after Marathon than himself. His sense of slight would have been heightened by his upbringing, for so much of male Greek life was posited as a competition: from the ways in which the epics and stories that young men had grown up with, like the Homeric epics, focused on the individual's desperate search for *kleos* and *time* – key Greek concepts of the honor paid in life and afterlife to the most successful individuals; to the gymnasiums where they had physically competed with one another; to the rough-and-tumble of political and military life and the honors and riches that went to the victors, often at expense of the losers. Winning was everything and losing out to others a crushing blow. But by this time Themistocles had seen examples of how individuals had risen again to prominence after falls from grace – if Athens needed them enough. The question was whether he too would be able to rise again.

But more bitter pills were to come for Themistocles to swallow. He had to watch as Aristides, the commander of the Athenian land forces at the Battle of Plataea, where the Persian army was routed and began its own mass exodus from Greece, was hailed as a hero. Just two years later, in 477, still trusted by the people of Athens, Aristides would be asked to conduct the first assessment of tribute from members of the new Delian League. This league was Athens's idea: a way to move from the defensive "Hellenic" league of Greek city-states, which had defended Greece against the Persian invasion, on to the offensive, taking the fight now to Persia and pressing the Greeks' advantage. It was in many ways the embodiment of what Themistocles had wanted to do immediately after Salamis. Sparta had no interest in leading an offensive campaign far from its own homeland, so Athens willingly took up the reins of the new Delian League, a modern-day name coined after the sacred island of Delos, in the heart of the Cyclades, where the twin gods Apollo and Artemis were said to have been born. It was on this tiny island that the oaths of alliance were sworn by members of the league and where the treasury of the Delian League was established. It was thus also to Delos that the moneys from its different members were sent, which Aristides – his ever-trustworthy reputation coming to the fore – was empowered to keep track of. Aristides' new successes as Themistocles' long-term contemporary rival and opponent prompted new levels of bitterness in Themistocles. In Plutarch's account of Aristides' life, he reports that Themistocles sniffed (no doubt in jealousy) at Aristides' role in the newly formed Delian League, responding to the praise given to Aristides for his honesty with the comment that that was praise more worthy of a safe-deposit box than a man.[15] Sour grapes indeed from someone who must have been furious at his long-term rival's success.

At the same time, the commander of the Athenian fleet, Xanthippus, also went on to greater glory following his part in the wider Greek fleet's success at Mycale, again doing exactly what Themistocles had started to do in the aftermath of Salamis. Xanthippus, elected eponymous archon in Athens for 479/8, and left in overall control of the remaining Athenian and Ionian ships after the Spartans and their allies sailed home following the destruction of the Persian fleet at Mycale, sailed to Sestus, a city on the European side of the Hellespont, where Xerxes had earlier crossed with his great army to attack. Indeed it was the first city Xerxes entered after he crossed the Hellespont, and so made a fitting candidate to be the first for the new offensive alliance led by Athens to visit. Xanthippus – mimicking what Themistocles had done to Andros – laid siege to the city and after several months forced it to surrender in the spring of 478. It was the first "success" of the Delian League, an alliance that would over the next thirty years gradually lead to the empire of Athens. The question was, would Themistocles, having been discarded so soon after his critical involvement in the Athenian victory at Salamis, have any role to play in his city's future triumphs?

CHAPTER NINE

The Hero Rises—And Falls (Again)

Themistocles was in Athens in the immediate aftermath of Plataea and Mycale. The city was still in ruins: there had been no time to systematically rebuild after Salamis, nor many able hands free to do so, given that the Athenian fighting men were either rowing the ships of the fleet or fighting on the battlefield. But after the Persian army went into retreat, the Athenians began to return home, and their minds turned to the rebuilding of their city. As Aristides, bathed in his reputation for justice and fairness, oversaw Athens's new proto-empire, and Xanthippus warmed to his new role as the tip of the Athenian imperial spear, Themistocles – perhaps channeling his bitterness and jealously as he sought a new way to be needed by the city of Athens – warmed to the idea of rebuilding the city at home very quickly indeed. Here, perhaps, was an area in which Athens needed strong leadership, a role that could allow Themistocles once again to prove his worth to the people and rise to prominence.

We might imagine that the Athenians would bc particularly keen to rebuild the symbolic center of their city, the Acropolis.

It stood dominant over the rest of the city, and its temples and statues to the gods, particularly the city's patron deity, Athena, had been smashed by the Persians. This was the place that the Athenians since time immemorial had come to celebrate their great victories – it was on the Acropolis, for instance, that the first military victories against the Boeotians and Chalcidians, secured under Cleisthenes' new political system of isonomia, were celebrated with the dedication of a grand statue group in the late sixth century BCE. There, too, new temples had been erected both by the tyrant rulers of Athens and by the government of the people in the early fifth century. Immediately after their victory at Marathon, the Athenians had started building a new grand temple that had required an extension of the Acropolis itself. The temple was half-built at the time of the Persian invasion in 480, but it too was reduced to ruins. It would have made sense for the Athenians to focus on ensuring that the sacred and historic heart of their city was returned to its former glory.

But they didn't. In fact, as far as we can tell from the historical sources and archaeological investigation, almost nothing was done on or around the Acropolis in the years – indeed, decades – after Plataea. A little sweeping up and burying of all the broken statues and pottery from the Acropolis seems to have occurred, so that the objects dedicated to, and thus belonging to, the gods were buried in the earth of the Acropolis and remained in the possession of the gods. But on the whole the ruins were left in ruins. This decision is explained in the later writings of the fourth-century BCE Athenian statesman Lycurgus and the first-century BCE chronographer Diodorus Siculus, who claim that an oath was taken by the people of Athens not to rebuild the heart of their city but leave the ruins "as a monument for men hereafter, a memorial of the impiety of the barbarians."[1] Impiety – in Greek, *asebeia* – was a serious charge reserved for those who had desecrated divine objects and shown irreverence toward the gods recognized by the state. It was for the Athenians the ultimate charge with which to define the base actions of the Persians.

Instead of restoring the Acropolis, the Athenians threw themselves into two key building projects – in both of which Themistocles is said to have had a strong hand. First, the city's circuit walls needed rebuilding to defend the city of Athens itself. This task seems to have taken priority over everything else, not simply over other areas of reconstruction but over any other task in which the Athenians were employed. And indeed, it took precedence over the survival of any other structure still standing or half-standing in their city. The historian Thucydides describes how "the whole population in the city was to labor at the wall, the Athenians, their wives and their children, sparing no edifice, private or public, which might be of any use to the work, but throwing all down."[2]

This might seem to be hyperbole. But Thucydides goes on to say that, especially in the foundations, the Athenians were encouraged to seize anything they could lay their hands on to build up the walls as quickly as possible. This included objects which usually would be considered untouchable: not just blocks of stone from private houses or ruined buildings, but even, especially in the areas where the walls ran past the graveyard of Athens in the area of Kerameikos, parts of grave markers and monuments were to be laid into the foundations. That the Athenians did this is confirmed by the archaeological findings: several older statues and stele that originally were set up as grave markers around Kerameikos were found buried in the city walls nearby. The Athenians, so says Thucydides, "laid their hands on everything without exception in their haste."[3]

What they created was a set of imposing walls running for some five miles around the city, up to thirty feet high and ten feet thick and punctuated by thirteen entrance gates. Plutarch is insistent that Themistocles was at the center of this rush to rebuild the city walls (to this day these walls are often referred to as the city's "Themistoclean walls"). Plutarch even goes so far as to report that Themistocles gave money to the men in authority at the time to ensure that the wall building was permitted and encouraged.[4]

But rebuilding the city walls was just one of the building projects Themistocles took a hand in. The other was the continued development, and now also securing, of the new harbor area of Piraeus. Back when he first emerged on the political scene in Athens as archon in 493/2, Themistocles was said to have encouraged the development of the three natural harbors at Piraeus as a superior base to that of Phaleron for the nascent Athenian navy. After the discovery of the massive silver seam at Laurion and its subsequent allocation to the construction of almost two hundred triremes, the requirement for an enlarged and superior port for Athens had become clear. Of course, the Athenian fleet had spent little time at any port in Athens itself in the period 480–478, instead harboring at Salamis, Andros, or farther afield. But now, as the head of the Delian League, Athens needed a harbor the fleet could come back to, as well as top-notch facilities for its upkeep and repair, and for the ongoing construction of more triremes. Over the next decades, Athens would double the size of its fleet to some four hundred triremes, a process that seems to have been begun under Themistocles. The Zea Harbour Project, run by the Danish Institute at Athens in conjunction with the Athenian ephorate, currently investigating the remains of the ancient shipsheds around one of the natural harbors of the larger Piraeus area, has identified at least fifteen new shipsheds constructed from 478 BCE onward in this area alone. These could have been used for building new triremes or for hauling older ones out of the water in order to repair them.[5]

The new engine room of Athenian naval power also needed protecting. It was in this period, during the 470s, that Piraeus itself was given protective walls, just like the city of Athens. Although the famous Long Walls, which connected the city of Athens to its port of Piraeus via a defensive corridor, would not be begun for another decade, it was in the 470s, and, at least according to the surviving later sources, under the strong influence of Themistocles, that the Athenians protected both their city and their harbor (and thus their fleet) with stout solid walls. In particular, the walls of Piraeus, while not as high as originally intended, were so thick that it was said two chariots could pass each other along them.

Why might Themistocles have been so eager to focus Athenian minds on improving their harbor and protecting both it and the city? Was it simply because the work provided an opportunity for him to emerge once again at center stage after being sidelined following Salamis? Or were there sound reasons for him to champion protective wall building and the expansion of the ports?

There were many good reasons for Themistocles to push these projects as a top priority for Athens in the years after the Persian invasion. On one hand, of course, he may have had an eye on preserving his legacy: the Athenian fleet and its new harbor at Piraeus. But on the other, he may also have understood how much had changed in the political atmosphere of Athens over the previous few years. He had come to prominence within a system of government based on isonomia, equality before the law. This was not quite the same as *demokratia*, people power. That term came into regular use to describe the Athenian system of government only at the end of the 470s and into the 460s (a popular boy's name of this period would be Demokrates!).[6] It might be thought that I am splitting hairs here between a system of isonomia and one of demokratia, but actually the differences ran deep. Equality before the law did not mean that anyone and everyone could or should be listened to in the Assembly, or indeed that every social class of citizen could or should be eligible for the highest political offices. Until 457 BCE, for example, only the top two property classes of Athenian citizens were eligible to be chosen as archon. Athens was also still some way off making it financially possible for every class of citizen to be actively involved in the public business of the city. In the 450s, the government introduced jury pay for men serving on juries in the people's courts, but it would not get around to introducing pay for those attending the Assembly until the 390s BCE. Thus, while its political system formally recognized equality before the law, Athens was, in the 470s, still far from being a system that enabled and championed the people as a whole holding power. Instead, as we have seen, influential figures still tended to come from wealthy families who had access to good education and independent income, which gave them the time to take part in politics, have access to the highest political offices, undertake the training and experience to do the job well, and (at least) sound as though they knew what they were talking about.

But the victory at Salamis brought a sea change in the balance of power. It was the first time that Athens's very survival had depended not on the wealthy elites who could afford to be part of the cavalry (with their expensive horses), or on the less wealthy "middle class" of Athenians who could afford the armor and weaponry of a hoplite, but on people who needed only to be able to row. Every citizen of Athens – irrespective of class, wealth, and education – had been able to contribute equally to the victory at Salamis and later to the increasingly powerful position of Athens within Greece more widely as it started to head up the Delian League. Realization of this people power had tsunami-like effects within Athens's political system through the remainder of the 470s and into the 460s, supercharging the polis's slow transformation into a system of demokratia across the following decade.

Plutarch indicates that Themistocles perhaps understood better than most the powerful impact that the victory at Salamis, and the increasing importance of the Athenian navy and its harbors, would have on Athens.[7] In building up Piraeus and ensuring that its protection was on a par with that of the city of Athens itself, he was both reflecting that change and encouraging it still further, by giving the fleet – and everything it symbolized – a more prestigious (and protected) physical base. From this point on, the radical democratic heartbeat of Athens was said to come from Piraeus rather than the *astu* – the city with the Acropolis at its heart – and during future internal civil strife within Athens, it was always from Piraeus that the democratic forces of Athens emerged strongest. Themistocles' actions were thus helping to propel democracy toward becoming a reality.

But there was another crucial motivation behind Themistocles' championing of the building of the city walls and the strengthening of Piraeus. This was not so much fear of a further invasion by the Persians, even though that was not by any means impossible. Rather it was the old fear that in the absence of a big external threat to Greece, the Greeks would once again do what they had always done: fight one another. And while Athens had a mighty fleet to give it dominance at sea, that was useless on land. Its land army was strong, but by no means the strongest in Greece, as the recent demonstrations of the valor of several Greek cities at Plataea, above all Sparta, had made clear. And a city without any walls to protect it was even more vulnerable. Had not the Spartans invaded Athens several times during its politically turbulent years at the end of the sixth century BCE in Themistocles' youth, before eventually being barricaded on the Acropolis and forced to leave? Rebuilding

Athens's city walls and creating defensive walls for Piraeus—and doing so in as much haste as possible—was a way for Athens to protect itself against its fellow Greeks.

But although Athens may have built the walls because it felt the need to protect itself, from the viewpoint of other Greek cities it looked as though Athens was building itself up to exert its authority over others and thus doing to them the same thing Athens may well have feared would be done to it. The other Greek cities were only too well aware of the degree to which they had been indebted to Athens's fleet at Salamis, as well as the way that fleet was leading the Delian League, moving around the Aegean and beginning to throw its weight around. Athens had also performed well on the battlefield at Plataea; its land army was not insignificant. And now it seemed to be building grand new city walls, preparing perhaps for further conflict.

Thucydides insightfully records these different perspectives on Athens's activity when he discusses Sparta's nomination by other Greek city-states (of the still existent Hellenic League, which had come together to resist the Persian invasion) to go to Athens at the first moment it became clear that Athens was thinking about rebuilding its city walls, in order to persuade them to leave them in ruins:

> They [the Spartans] would have themselves preferred to see neither her [Athens] nor any other city in possession of a wall; though here they acted principally at the instigation of their allies, who were alarmed at the strength of her newly acquired navy, and the valor which she had displayed in the war with the Persians. The Spartans begged her not only to abstain from building walls for herself, but also to join them in throwing down the city walls that still survived of cities outside the Peloponnese.[8]

The public argument as to why this should be done was not the general fear of Athens but rather that if Greece were to be invaded again, the enemy would be denied a secure base if there were no cities with walls in mainland Greece, and that all the Greeks, having evacuated their defenseless cities, could find refuge in the well-protected (and walled) cities of the Peloponnese, which could be defended at the Isthmus.

Sparta could make this argument without being labeled hypocritical because its city had never had walls: within Spartan culture and ideology, its male citizen soldiers had been considered all the walls Sparta would ever need – if an enemy were ever to get close enough to the city in the first place. But neither Themistocles nor the Athenians (nor, surely, most of the other Greek cities) were convinced that they should all pull down their walls and live in mutually assured vulnerability, with the cities of the Peloponnese as their only place of refuge. It was after the Spartans had left that Themistocles is said to have urged every Athenian to turn to wall building as quickly as possible. And at the same time, Themistocles himself reportedly played a key role in giving Athens the breathing space it needed to finish its city walls before any other Greek city-state could move against it.

The best way to do that: pretend the walls were not being built. Plutarch, Thucydides, and others explain that Themistocles arranged for himself to be sent as ambassador to Sparta (he made a good candidate, given the recent honors the Spartans had bestowed on him).[9] Having delayed his visit until the walls were well under way, he then slowly made his way to Sparta. Once there, he kept making excuses for not formally appearing before the Spartan officials, saying that he was waiting for his fellow ambassadors, who were delayed on some other business, to arrive. (He had actually told them not to come until the Athenian walls were high enough to defend the city.)

The Spartans believed Themistocles until reports from other cities started to reach them of the significant wall building at Athens. They challenged Themistocles, at which point, still studiously denying that the Athenians were building walls, Themistocles suggested the Spartans send a delegation to Athens to check for themselves. At the same time, he sent messages back to Athens saying that the Spartan delegation should be detained (in the politest way possible) until he and his fellow ambassadors arrived: in effect the Spartan embassy was to be held hostage in order to ensure Themistocles' release when the deception came fully to light.

Themistocles' fellow ambassadors arrived in Sparta in due course to confirm to Themistocles that the city's wall was high and strong, and it was only then that Themistocles admitted to the Spartans that the Athenians had already built a city wall and thought it in their best interest to do so. He made the simple point that Athens could not have an equal voice in the debates of the Greeks if it did not have military strength equal to that of the rest of the Greeks, including city walls. So either every Greek city (even those in the Peloponnese) needed to take down its walls, or the Spartans – and everyone else – would just have to accept what Athens had done. The Spartans could do little but let Themistocles go and secure the return of their own ambassadors. Perhaps they realized that the man they had crowned for his cleverness and cunning had proved his worth.

This must have been a proud moment for Themistocles, as he found himself once again at the epicenter of Athenian affairs, providing strong leadership for Athens at the same time he boldly stood up to the demands of other Greek cities. The audacity he had shown at Salamis – risking his life by engaging in a deception in order to bring about what he was sure was the right course of action – was once again on display as he put himself at the forefront of both the deception of, and subsequent negotiations with, Sparta.

Yet Themistocles' audacity stretched even farther this time. Once back in Athens, noting that the rest of the allied Greek fleet, following the destruction of the Persians at Mycale, had put in at the port of Pagasae for the winter, he ventured to suggest to the Athenian Assembly a plan to bring additional advantage to the city. Realizing its sensitive nature, he said he could not publicly reveal what his plan was. The Assembly told Themistocles to describe his plan to Aristides, and if he thought it wise they would happily enact it. Themistocles suggested to Aristides that the Athenian fleet should sail out and burn the rest of the allied Greek fleet. With all Greece but Athens fleet-less, and the Athenians all-powerful with their triremes at sea and their walls to protect them at home, Athens would be in pole position to become the dominant city in maritime Greece. This was exactly what the other Greek city-states had feared that Athens's wall building heralded: a new level of inter-Greek conflict.

Aristides told the Assembly that Themistocles' plan was simultaneously of the upmost advantage to Athens and at the same time a most unjust course of action. Aristides had it summed up correctly. In many ways Themistocles had taken his experiences of the campaign at Salamis – his perception of the ultimate lack of loyalty of Greeks to one another and their persistent willingness to abandon each other to save themselves unless they had no option but to remain together – and applied it in reverse to Athens's newfound position of power. Without fleets of their own, the other city-states would have no option but to follow Athens's lead. His plan would have once again forced Greek unity, but a unity in which the rest of Greece accepted Athens as its master rather than as another member of a league or alliance. It was an assessment lacking in empathy and a sense of fair play, but it was not out of keeping given Themistocles' previous actions, such as when he forced the Greeks to fight at Salamis. The Athenian Assembly, however, at the direction of Aristides, told Themistocles to drop the plan. And for once he is said to have followed orders, without trying to manipulate events behind the scenes.

Athens was, however, not the only city attempting to improve its position within the Greek world at this time. Sparta was too. We have already seen how Sparta had suggested to Themistocles that all cities outside the Peloponnese should tear down their walls, leaving only cities inside the Peloponnese able to protect themselves. And while Sparta's intentions may not have been wholly selfish, they definitely did reflect a desire to ensure that the Peloponnese (with Sparta at its heart) was the ultimate refuge and strong place of Greece.

A similar effort to ensure a powerful voice for the Spartans (and the others who had fought with them against the Persians) on the wider Greek stage was seen soon after the walls incident. One of the historic ways in which the Greeks had come together before the alliance that had stood against the Persians was through the Amphictyonic Council. This was a grouping of cities and states from across Greece that were technically responsible for two sanctuaries: the sanctuary of Demeter at Anthela, in Thessaly, and, after the "First Sacred War" of the sixth century BCE, the sanctuary of Apollo at Delphi. It was the importance of this sanctuary, which by the 470s had become the preeminent oracular sanctuary in Greece and self-declared "common hearth of the Greeks," that gave the Amphictyonic Council, which oversaw it and met at it, significant authority. The Spartans now proposed to exclude any city or state that was a member of the Amphictyony but had not fought in the alliance against the Persians. Plutarch tells us that

Themistocles again saw the danger of this key council suddenly becoming the preserve of the Spartans (and its allies), and he managed to persuade the delegates to turn down Sparta's suggestion on the basis that a council with so few representatives, and with the rest of Greece excluded, would have given too much power to those remaining representatives. It was an ironic argument to say the least, given his suggestion that the Athenians burn the fleets of the rest of Greece. He seemed to have no problem with the idea of Athenian supremacy, just with the supremacy of any other city.

It was perhaps not a difficult task to convince the others that the Spartans' plans to stack the deck in their favor should be resisted. More widely across the Aegean, the Spartan commander Pausanias had recently been throwing his weight around, with expeditions against Cyprus and Byzantium (modern-day Istanbul). But, worse, he had also been very heavy-handed – indeed, some complained, tyrannical – in his dealings with fellow Greeks. He was recalled to Sparta to face charges, but it was this heavy-handedness that had encouraged first the Ionians to ask the Athenians to lead them and subsequently the remaining allied city-states to lose confidence in Sparta as their overall commander and to ask Athens to lead the alliance that would now take the fight to Persia in the form of the Delian League.

The Spartans, it is said, at the point when their plans for the Amphictyonic Council were turned down, lost all faith in Themistocles as a friend of Sparta. They had given him public recognition for his wisdom and cunning, and he had now duped them about Athens's wall building and publicly opposed them in the council. Sparta began to befriend, and actively support, other leading figures in Athens, above all Cimon, the son of Miltiades, who would soon become Themistocles' greatest rival.[10] Themistocles was running out of allies who would recognize his worth.

Themistocles, according to Plutarch, liked to claim that the Athenians did not honor or admire him but treated him like a plane tree: "They ran beneath his branches when there was a storm and they were in danger of getting drenched, but when they had a period of fine weather, they plucked and pruned him."[11] He had some reason to make this claim: he had been the architect of the victory at Salamis (if not perhaps the sole architect) but had been dropped as the Athenian naval commander the following year. He was given no formal official role in the new Delian League, and although he rose to prominence again in the discussions and activities surrounding the rebuilding of Athens's walls at a time when Athens needed protection, he afterward played little formal role in the official politics of the day. Yet it is clear from his tree metaphor that Themistocles' view of strong leaders in Athens was very different from that which his father had once used to warn him off politics. His father had shown him the rotting ships that had been abandoned once they were of no use. For his father, leaders in Athens had a finite time to lead before being permanently abandoned and left to decay. For Themistocles, the view was different. He was a massive, strong tree, a living, growing, unmovable, and unforgettable part of the landscape. There would be times when the Athenians took shelter under him and times when they pruned him. But in Themistocles' view, there was no end to that cycle, no shelf life, as for a ship. He was plucked and pruned but never cut down. He was a tree that kept on living and growing in an endless cycle within the epicenter of power politics at Athens.

It was perhaps this belief that he was a more permanent part of the Athenian landscape, subject to an ongoing cycle of honor and exclusion, that tipped Themistocles into misjudging his fellow Athenians. Perhaps out of boredom, or out of annoyance at not being as honored as he would have liked to be, or in an attempt to take control of the cycle and reinsert himself as central to Athenian political and military affairs, Themistocles forgot the central lesson of Athenian politics – the importance of seeming to care more about the city than for oneself – and continued to actively remind everyone of how much they owed him. In 477, he had sponsored a tragic play at the City Dionysia by Phrynichus that alluded to the crushing of the Persian fleet at Salamis – a play which obviously reflected his own greatest achievements. The play is said to have won the dramatic contest, after which Themistocles erected a votive plaque in Athens commemorating his victory. To those who complained, he expressed disbelief that they could tire of receiving benefits so often from the same person.[12]

If reminders of his prowess in public places like the theater did not rapidly increase the annoyance, jealousy, and intolerance of the citizen body of Athens, then Themistocles' next move most certainly would have done, for it was impossible to avoid it. Themistocles lived in central Athens in the deme of Melite, which lay just west of the Acropolis, within the city walls.[13] Most important, in this deme were sited key public places and organs of the democracy: the Agora and the Pnyx, where the Athenian Assembly met. Melite was quickly becoming an important religious center, home not simply to the temples and altars of the Agora but also, since 476/5, of a grand new Theseion, shrine to Theseus, an early king of Athens and now an Athenian hero par excellence. In fact it had been Cimon, Themistocles' Spartan-backed rival, who had gone to the island of Skyros to recover the bones of Theseus where they had been buried. He returned them triumphantly to Athens, and they were reburied at the heart of a new shrine covered in paintings by the leading artists of the day that illustrated Theseus's adventures in Crete as well as great mythical conflicts of civilization versus "barbarism." This shrine to Theseus was brand new in the mid-470s when Themistocles chose to build a new shrine within the deme of Melite near his home. But Themistocles' shrine was not erected to worship a great Athenian hero of the past, around whom the whole community could gather and identify themselves. This shrine was dedicated to the goddess Artemis, with the epithet "Aristoboule," "Best Counselor." If the location of the shrine – near his house – did not make it clear whom he thought Artemis had inspired with the best counsel for the Athenians, then the portrait of Themistocles which was said to have stood in the temple up until the time of Plutarch left little room for doubt.

From archaeological excavation we know that the structure itself was modest: just twelve square feet. But it was located in a highly visible site at the junction of two important roads (one coming from the Agora to the Peiraic Gate of the city walls and the other leading to the Demian Gate), within a thriving deme of the city, close to the vital sites of the democracy itself: the Agora and the Pnyx.[14] Along with Themistocles' other actions, it is no wonder the Athenians' patience started to run thin. And for a man awarded the prize for wisdom, who considered himself to be the receiver and channeler of Artemis's wisdom and counsel, the building of the temple and its association with himself was a spectacular miscalculation of what a political system that he himself had helped bring into being would accept. Themistocles had demonstrated the ultimate hubris of Athenian politics: he had made himself the key issue.

In 472, Themistocles received, obliquely, some of the praise he had been looking for, in Aeschylus's play *The Persians,* performed as part of the City Dionysia. In it, the playwright, who himself fought at Marathon, echoed the idea that Themistocles was central to Athens's success at Salamis – but, crucially, he did so without formally mentioning Themistocles' name.[15] But how fast things could change. Plutarch recounts that as the actions of Themistocles – particularly his shrine building – started to grate on the Athenians, and the jealously and annoyance at the way Themistocles continued to demand high honor continued to grow, the Athenians became more and more willing to listen to claims of his wrongdoing.[16] Plutarch and others later record an infamous brag of Themistocles' son that no doubt also found willing ears during this time. The son would say publicly that whatever pleased him pleased all of Athens, for whatever he liked, his mother liked, and what his mother liked, his father liked, and whatever Themistocles liked, Athens liked.[17] All this anger and envy were no doubt stoked further by the old aristocratic elite families, who were united in opposition to Themistocles, in particular the Alcmaeonids, who had been for some time allied through marriage with another powerful set of elites led by Cimon and his family. (Cimon, in turn, was being actively supported by Sparta.) A year after Aeschylus's play was performed, plentiful surviving ostraca from the ostracism vote of 471 bear Themistocles' name – in fact, far more than for any other candidate.[18] Themistocles was banished from Athens.

CHAPTER TEN

Reinvention

Themistocles probably considered his ostracism something of a temporary setback. On one hand, ostracism lasted technically for ten years – a not inconsiderable time. But on the other, many ostracisms, like those of his long-term political rivals Aristides and Xanthippus, had been cut much shorter in times of need. And those who had been ostracized and then returned had also subsequently regained important roles within the city: Aristides oversaw the Delian treasury and Xanthippus led its fleet. If Themistocles were the plane tree for the Athenians to hide beneath in times of crisis, a permanent part of the Athenian landscape, then all that was needed was another crisis – and, crucially, another need that he could present himself as filling. His experience of the constant rise and fall of individuals in Athenian politics, his sense of himself as a strong, living, growing part of the Athenian landscape, probably indicated to him that he would have further opportunities. Perhaps he even had time to reflect and recognize his own role in this latest cycle of honor and exclusion, having publicly valued himself above the Athenian collective, and thus learned how not to do things in the future if—or, rather, when—he was given another chance.

What he had not reckoned on was the Spartans. They were no longer interested in supporting Themistocles, who had tricked them over the Athenians' walls, both because they had found a new Athenian champion in his rival Cimon, and also because Themistocles, having been ostracized, had based himself in the city of Sparta's main rival, Argos. Yet it was more than the Spartans' hostility toward Themistocles that would prove harmful. In the time that Themistocles had been focused on trying to ensure his own political future in Athens, the Spartans had been attempting to contain a problem of their own that would now come to haunt Themistocles in exile. The Spartan general Pausanias, who had been recalled because of his heavy-handedness in the aftermath of the Persian retreat, had been tried for treason but found not guilty. He was a free man. And as a free man he sailed back to the Hellespont. Thucydides tells us that his goal was to pursue an alliance with the Persian King, which he had initiated when he captured Byzantium while he was still holding Spartan office. Hearing that he was up to no good once more, even in a private capacity, the Spartans sent a ship to bring him back to Sparta, where he was thrown in prison and tried again. Eventually evidence came forward of his attempt to collude with Xerxes. Pausanias managed to escape the authorities and seek sanctuary within Sparta's principal temple, thinking himself therefore untouchable, since the authorities could not cause harm in a sacred place for fear of angering the gods. They did not touch him—they instead literally walled him up inside the temple and starved him. He finally gave himself up, but he was so weak that he died just outside the shrine.[1]

How did this affect Themistocles? The Spartans, in finally uncovering Pausanias's dealings with the Persian King, came across evidence that Themistocles might be involved as well. Of course, because they were no friends of Themistocles, they took the evidence to Athens and recommended that the Athenians punish him. Their story, as told by Plutarch, was that Pausanias, when he saw Themistocles had been ostracized, invited him to join in his alliance with the Persian King, urging him "to turn against the Greeks as a worthless and ungrateful people." According to Plutarch, Themistocles rejected the advances but also did not tell anyone about Pausanias's plans.[2]

The Athenians – and particularly those in Athens keen to see any hope Themistocles might have of returning to Athenian politics quashed – were concerned about these latest accusations. But Themistocles was already ostracized and no longer in Athens. Plutarch tells us that Themistocles took these latest accusations very seriously: he wrote a public letter to the Athenians defending himself and arguing that since they had ostracized him because he was trying to rule the people of Athens, why would they think he would accept the rule of the Persian King? The Athenians were not convinced. It is no surprise that it was a member of the Alcmaeonid family called Leobotes who formally proposed a charge of treason against him. In around 468, the Athenians sent a delegation of citizens along with some Spartans, who were happy to oblige, to arrest Themistocles in Argos and bring him back to Athens for a formal trial.[3] The speed with which Themistocles had gone from being the hero of Salamis to an overlooked Athenian former general to supreme wall builder and defender of Athens to ostracized outsider and finally to a defendant on trial for treason topped anything Athens had seen over the previous decades. It was the ultimate example of how fickle the Athenian people, and the Athenian system, could be – but also perhaps an illustration of how focused on people power that system was becoming. No one could presume to have the people's favor who did not deliver for the people, and no one was safe if the people suspected he did not have their best interests at heart.

Themistocles got wind of his forthcoming arrest through some of his remaining supporters in Athens and left Argos before his pursuers could arrive. Trying to defend his name was one thing, leaving himself prey to the machinations of a treason trial in Athens was another thing entirely. He had seen at first hand how that had turned out for Miltiades. Heading out into the Corinthian Gulf, he sailed up the west coast of Greece to the island of Corcyra (modern-day Corfu), where he believed he would be safe because of his previous good deeds for the island, including acting as arbiter in a quarrel Corcyra had with Corinth (and deciding in the island's favor!). But the Corcyreans were afraid of the Athenians and Spartans and so deposited him on the mainland coast of northern Greece in Epirus.[4] Themistocles was suddenly in a very different world, not a patchwork of city-states, but a patchwork of different *ethne,* tribal groupings and kingdoms ruled over by hereditary monarchs, all of whom had seen the Persians sweep down past them through Greece and had had to make their own arrangements for their survival. None of these people owed Themistocles anything.

Themistocles came to the court of King Admetus of the Molossians, one of the ethne groupings within Epirus in northwestern Greece. The king was not at the palace, so Themistocles apparently received an audience with his wife. According to Thucydides, Themistocles explained his situation and formally asked as a suppliant for the Molossians' protection. Admetus's wife handed him her baby and told him to sit by the hearth with the babe in arms. When Admetus returned, he found Themistocles in what the Molossians saw as the most reverent position for a suppliant: sitting by a hearth with a child in his arms. Admetus was an honorable man, and although he and Themistocles had disagreed over the relationship between the Molossians and the Athenians in the past, he could not overlook this direct and potent act of supplication. When the Spartans and the Athenians, pursuing Themistocles from Argos to Corcyra and finally to the court of Admetus, arrived, Admetus refused to hand him over to them. It was to Epirus that Themistocles' remaining friends in Athens were able to smuggle his wife and children so as to reunite the family (although we do not know whether the wife was his first wife or whether he had already remarried).[5]

But Themistocles could not stay forever at Admetus's court. By this time, Themistocles had been condemned to death for treason in absentia by the courts of Athens. Diodorus Siculus even claims that the Spartans threatened to unite the Greeks in a war against Admetus if he did not turn Themistocles over to them.[6] Themistocles' options were now limited. Between them Sparta and Athens could count on the compliance (by force or by mutual agreement) of the majority of Greek city-states and tribal kingdoms – the two were, respectively, the greatest land power and the greatest sea power in the Greek world. Even if Themistocles did find a Greek city-state or kingdom that would defy Athens and Sparta and protect him, he might be safe for a limited period, but it would not be a permanent solution to his problem, as eventually that city-state or kingdom would have to bow to the pressure to hand him over. He was beginning to realize that if he returned to Athens to fight for his reputation, there was no certainty that he would win. In fact, even if he were to overturn his death penalty and it be reduced again to mere ostracism, there was unlikely to be a future for him in Athens, even after his period of ostracism ended. He had been tarnished by the accusation of being in league with the Persian King at a time when Greece, and particularly Athens, was ever more ferociously defining Greekness as the antithesis of everything Persian. The war against Persia and the resulting Greek victory, which Themistocles had done so much to bring about, had created a cultural sea change in Greece. Anything Persian was now seen as antithetical to what Greece was and wanted to be. The Persians were *barbaroi*, "barbarians," the opposite of "civilized" Greeks. Everything connected with the Persians – the way they behaved, the cultural values they held, the way they dressed, the way they engaged with the outside world, the gods they worshipped, even the way they spoke (*barbaroi* at its root means those who speak nonsense) – was regarded as inferior, weak, effeminate, anti-freedom, and just plain wrong. In that atmosphere, a man charged with plotting in league with the Persian King had few defenses. Themistocles' sense of himself as a plane tree – a strong, ever-living element in the Athenian landscape – was fast withering at the root.

The solution that presented itself to Themistocles (or, according to Diodorus Siculus, that he was persuaded to adopt by Admetus) might have seemed, at first, equally unthinkable: to go to the Persian court and secure the protection of the King of Persia.[7] But this was a course that a number of prominent Greeks had taken in recent decades when their options in Greece had run out. Themistocles was well aware that Hippias, the former tyrant of Athens, who had been forced out of the city in the revolution of 510, had sought refuge with the Persian King and, indeed, accompanied the Persian forces in 490, in the hope of being reinstated, when they had attacked at Marathon. After the attack failed, Hippias had lived out his days in the service of the Persian ruler. But he was joined after 490 by another Greek, Demaratus, who until 491 had been one of the kings of Sparta. Ousted from his rule in a plot by his fellow king (Sparta had two kings at a time in this period), he too, with no other city willing to give him sanctuary in Greece, had fled to the Persian King and received a warm reception, being given cities and lands in western Asia Minor (around the later city of Pergamon) to rule over.

Demaratus had continued to advise King Darius and his son Xerxes about dealing with the Greeks, and he had accompanied Xerxes on his subsequent invasion of Greece in 480–479, repeatedly (so Herodotus has it) warning Xerxes not to underestimate the fighting strength of the Greeks and particularly the Spartans. In the wake of the failure of the expedition, Demaratus returned to Persia. Yet another Greek had also arrived seeking the support and welcome of the Persian King, a man called Gongylus from Eretria on Euboea. Gongylus had previously acted as an intermediary between Sparta and Xerxes. Pausanias, the Spartan general whose association with Themistocles had caused the latter's downfall in Athens, had also, of course, at various times in his career sought the support of the Persian King. Themistocles thus was not so much grasping at straws as taking a path that others had trodden before him – some very recently.[8] But none of the other Greeks had been so obviously – and successfully – pitted against the Persian King in battle, or had personally sought to deceive him. Themistocles was not just a Greek seeking refuge in Persia, he was an active and known enemy of Persia and its King now seeking refuge in Persia.

The journey to Persia was itself fraught with difficulties. Admetus helped him (and possibly paid for him) to cross northern Greece from Epirus to the court of King Alexander of Macedon on the northeastern side of mainland Greece. There, at the seaport of Pydna, not far from modern-day Thessaloniki, Themistocles sought out a ship that would take him across the Aegean to the coast of Asia Minor (we do not know whether his wife and children traveled with him). It was a hazardous journey, given the powerful Athenian fleet that now prowled these waters in the name of the Delian League. He traveled throughout in disguise, knowing that if he were discovered, allegiance to Sparta or Athens would lead to his arrest. Themistocles' ship set sail with no one on board recognizing him—and Themistocles hoped to keep it that way. But then a storm blew up near Naxos, and the merchant vessel needed to head for safety into the port, which was currently being blockaded by the Athenian fleet. In desperation, Themistocles revealed himself to the ship's captain and promised him a substantial reward if he would keep the ship away from the Athenian fleet. That reward came together with a threat: if Themistocles were discovered, he would tell the Athenians that the captain was knowingly transporting him to Persia, for which the captain would be punished. The captain decided to chance it, rode out the storm at anchor away from the Athenian fleet, and reached the coast of Asia Minor. To Themistocles' credit, at least according to Thucydides, he arranged for friends of his in Athens and Argos to send this captain his promised reward.[9]

By this time, sometime after 468, Themistocles was in his late fifties. As he stood on the coast of Asia Minor, he knew he was at—or in many ways already past—the point of no return. The Athenians and Spartans had chased him around Greece, and the mood in Athens had resolutely turned against him as a defendant who had fled his trial and been condemned to death for treason. Plutarch records that his property was in the process of being officially confiscated by the Athenian state, something that was not done to those who were simply serving out a period of ostracism. Confiscation was confined to convicted criminals. The temple Themistocles had helped construct, the Temple of Artemis Aristoboule, seems, according to the archaeological evidence, to have been left to fall into disrepair. His remaining friends in Athens were said to have spirited away as much as they could of his money and belongings to send to him in Asia, but the Athenian treasury reportedly took possession of a fortune of over a hundred talents – enough to build roughly a hundred triremes. Not a bad fortune for a man who, according to Plutarch, started his adult political career with no more than three talents of property.[10]

But it was probably what waited ahead of him that was preoccupying Themistocles more than what lay behind. He had taken the risk of going to Persia, but he still had to convince the Persian King to give him sanctuary. Even getting to the king in order to put his case was no easy task. It was not simply the geographical distance he might have to travel from the coast inland to the heart of Persia wherever the King was to be found, or the layers of bureaucracy he might have to go through in order to secure an audience. Themistocles was an Athenian – an enemy – exposed and alone in Persian territory. Anyone learning of his identity might turn on him at any moment. One false move could be his last.

Plutarch tells us that Themistocles was in danger on Persian soil not simply because he was an Athenian but because he was Themistocles: the leader of the Athenians at Salamis and thus a personal enemy of the King. In fact, he had a bounty of two hundred talents on his head. To avoid recognition, Themistocles headed from the coast of Asia Minor where he had landed as secretly as he could to Aegae, a small town in Aeolis (near where Pergamon would in centuries to come grow into a famous center of power). In this small town, Themistocles was, according to Plutarch, unknown to anyone except the one person he himself knew there, one Nicogenes.[11] Nicogenes was the wealthiest man in Aeolis and well known to (and respected by) the King's court. Nicogenes offered Themistocles shelter, despite the price on his head and the potential repercussions for himself and his family. We do not know how Themistocles persuaded him, beyond, perhaps, banking on the cultural importance Greeks laid on showing hospitality to guests and particularly to those who supplicated for support and assistance (a ploy that had worked well with his friend Admetus).

Themistocles stayed in hiding with Nicogenes for several days, but Plutarch recounts that he was initially without a plan about where to go next. This sounds unlike the Themistocles we have come to expect from the later sources: the quick-witted, audacious, far-sighted individual, ever-ready to turn a situation to his advantage, someone who never panicked. But Plutarch alludes to Themistocles being in a state of "desperate terror and panic." It is perhaps the most human picture of Themistocles we see in the whole of Plutarch's account: a man alone, in hiding, in the vastness of an empire he has been instrumental in defeating in battle, and on the run from his homeland, which has turned against him. No wonder Plutarch recounts that Themistocles dreamed of a snake winding up along his body toward his neck.[12]

That same snake in Themistocles' dream, however, turned into an eagle that carried him to safety – an omen which may well have given Themistocles the courage to continue. But whereas Thucydides merely recounts that Themistocles "proceeded inland with one of the Persians," in Plutarch's Life of Themistocles we hear more of the subterfuge employed to enable him to do so. For whatever Nicogenes' standing, he could not simply travel openly across Persia to the King's court with Themistocles by his side. Instead, it was Nicogenes, according to Plutarch, who came up with the ingenious solution of hiding Themistocles within a tented wheeled wagon, usually reserved in Persia for the transport of women, which prevented outsiders from seeing who was inside. The staff that accompanied the wagon was ordered to tell anyone who asked that inside was a young Greek woman from Ionia being sent to become one of the King's concubines.[13]

What we think happened next depends again on which ancient source we choose to favor. The first issue is which Persian King Themistocles sought to persuade. Thucydides believed that Themistocles did not have the opportunity to present himself to the King until after Xerxes, the ruler whom he had fought against at Salamis, died, and that Themistocles instead sought the favor of Xerxes' son Artaxerxes I. However, Plutarch reports that several other ancient historians believed that Themistocles arrived at the Persian court while Xerxes was still on the throne. Xerxes was said to have spent much of his time after his return from Greece focused on completing building projects begun by his father at Susa and Persepolis. But in 465, the commander of the royal bodyguard, Artabanus, led a plot to assassinate Xerxes and may also have murdered Xerxes' eldest son and heir, whereupon the commander of the royal bodyguard and his family were murdered by Xerxes' younger son. Alternatively, the commander may have accused Xerxes' eldest son of murdering his own father, at which point the younger son then murdered the older one before also killing the commander and his family.[14] The younger son, Artaxerxes, then took the throne to reestablish and consolidate Achaemenid control.

Thus we have either to imagine a slower progression for Themistocles from Greece after his condemnation for treason in 468 toward his engagement with the Persian King after 465, or to imagine him arriving at the Persian court before 465 and having to persuade the very king he had confronted, misinformed, and defeated in battle.[15] But which Persian King Themistocles sought to persuade is not the only difference in the versions of the story handed down to us. Equally at odds are the ways in which Themistocles is said to have made his case.

Thucydides has a version in which we see a more reserved and hesitant Themistocles: he does not seek a personal audience with the King, but instead sends him a letter. In it he acknowledges that he has done the Persians great harm, but claims that he has also done them a great favor, especially in giving them advance warning of the Greeks' intention to cut off their retreat home after Salamis. And for this, he claims, he deserves a return, but he adds that he can also offer further good service to the Persians. Additionally, the letter claims that he does not want to come before the King without being able to speak to him directly in Persian. So he asks to be allowed a year to live safely in Persia, learn Persian, and then come to speak with him. Thucydides tells us that the Persian King was impressed with Themistocles' *dianoia,* meaning both his "purpose" and his "willingness and desire to engage," but also perhaps with his intelligence and courage. In this account, Themistocles was given a year's grace to live in Persia and learn Persian.[16]

Plutarch offers us a more courageous version of Themistocles. Having traveled to the King's court in the tented wagon, he secured a meeting with the same head of the King's bodyguard who would later assassinate Xerxes: Artabanus the Chiliarch (grand vizier). Perhaps Themistocles achieved this by asking one of his wives, a woman from Eretria in Greece, to secure the interview for him. But he refused to tell Artabanus his name, saying only that he was a Greek and that he wished to have an audience with the King. Artabanus's reply was to first assess whether this Greek would recognize that he was in a different country, which worked by different rules and customs. He told Themistocles that if he wanted an audience directly with the King, he would need to prostrate himself in front of the King, as this was the standard behavior for all Persians. If he would not do that, then he would be able only to send messages to the King.

Themistocles was faced with the ultimate choice: risk surrendering his life or abandon his own Greek customs, and do what the Persian King had sought to force all Greece to do and which he had fought hard to prevent, in order to be able to make his case directly to the King. Themistocles' answer, according to Plutarch, was unequivocal. Not only was he in Persia, and thus obligated adopt Persian customs, but he had come to increase the fame and power of the King and, in time, to ensure that more men prostrated themselves before him as a result.

Plutarch thus suggests that Themistocles was able to secure a direct audience with the Persian King without ever revealing his name. In front of the King he did prostrate himself and then, according to Plutarch, through an interpreter he advanced the same arguments as those contained in Thucydides' letter: that he had done both great harm to and a great favor for the Persians, and that now he offered his services to them. He underlined that the Greeks had turned on him and driven him out: he was now their enemy – and their enemy was Persia's friend. The Persian King is said not have replied directly but to have rejoiced privately not only in Themistocles' bold approach but in the hope that more of his enemies would end up driving out their best leaders to him. The next day, Themistocles was made to return – having probably spent the night wondering whether the biggest gamble of his life would pay off or lead to his immediate execution. In the event, he found himself in front of a King willing not only to speak to him directly but also to give him the two hundred-talent bounty for having turned himself in, and a year to learn Persian so that they could talk properly together.[17]

In his mid- to late fifties, depending on when Themistocles had his audience with one of the Kings, Themistocles embarked on an entirely new life – one for which he had to learn a new language, acquire new customs, and develop new friendships and alliances, all the while ensuring that he kept the goodwill of the Persian King.[18] In many ways this could be seen as an absolute willingness to abandon principles in a desperate attempt to survive. But in other ways, Themistocles was returning to his roots as something of an outsider. He had been brought up in an ambiguous position within Greek society and spent much of his early life trying to establish himself within a system which had labeled him alien. Now as an adult he was doing the same thing. And perhaps the experiences of his youth stood him in good stead and enabled him once again to become an insider in his new world. Indeed, despite being one of a number of Greeks throughout the Classical period who came to the King's court, he is the only one known to have properly learned to speak Persian. He understood – perhaps better than most – the degree to which one had to go to fit in and become part of the system.[19]

Thucydides and Plutarch agree that this latest transition was indeed a success. Thucydides goes as far as to say that Themistocles became more important in the Persian court than any Greek had hitherto been owing to his intelligence and wit, but also in part by continually keeping alive in the Persian King's mind the hope of one day subduing the Greeks. Plutarch suggests that he was welcomed into the King's inner circle, speaking with the King often alone (since he spoke Persian and did not require an interpreter), going on the King's hunt, meeting with female members of the King's family, being instructed in the doctrines of the Magi in a way that no Greek or other foreigner had previously been invited to do. The irony, perhaps, is that the linguistic skill of persuasion (and indeed trickery) which had enabled him to do so much during his career in Athens, was equally effective in his new language, once again enabling him to achieve great things.[20]

He was also made a newly – or rather even more – wealthy man because of his friendship with the King. As was the custom for those in favor, cities were allocated to him to rule over and to supply him with his needs: Lampsacus, Magnesia, and Myus, scattered along the western Asia Minor coast. He came eventually to settle in grand luxury in Magnesia, farther south from where his Greek-now-Persian "contemporaries" had settled: Gongylus was ruling in the territory of Pergamon, and Demaratus ruled over cities nearby. Perhaps being a little distant from his fellow Greeks was no bad thing, and there was probably little love lost among this Athenian, a Spartan, and an Eretrian. But that did not mean that Themistocles refused to help out his fellow Greeks in times of need. On one occasion, Demaratus is said to have been told to choose a gift for himself from the Persian King. He asked to enter the city of Sardis and ride through it in celebration, wearing the same tiara worn by the King. Wanting to imitate the King was an overreaching request from someone who served the King. Instead of receiving his gift, Demaratus was expelled from the ruler's company. But Plutarch tells us that Themistocles intervened on Demaratus's behalf to reconcile him to the King. His actions clearly worked: the descendants of Demaratus would continue to rule over his cities through the rest of the fifth and into the fourth century BCE (as would the descendants of Gongylus nearby).[21]

When not supporting his fellow Greeks, Themistocles seems to have been charged by the King, as he is said to have promised, with resolving the "Greek problem" – that is to say, helping him figure out how the Persians could eventually conquer Greece (picking up perhaps from Demaratus, who had previously been lead adviser). This was no easy feat: the Greeks, led by the Athenians (and the Athenians were led in turn by their new, popular leader Cimon), had taken the fight proactively to Persia as part of the creation of the Delian League. This culminated in about 466, just before Themistocles left Greece to establish himself in Persia, in the Battle of Eurymedon, by a river on the southern coast of Asia Minor. The Persians had gathered a significant fleet there, with a view to beginning a new conquest of the Aegean islands and then perhaps mainland Greece. Cimon, on hearing of these preparations, had sailed to the area with the Athenian-led Greek fleet and directly engaged the Persians, sailing into the mouth of the river Eurymedon from the sea. His quick destruction of much of the Persian fleet allowed him to land his troops and achieve an equally decisive victory over the land forces built up there. The Aegean was once more under Greek control, and a major offensive by the Persians against Greece would have required starting from square one.

But in the immediate aftermath of Artaxerxes' bloody accession to the throne in 465, whatever he may have desired, conquest of Greece could not be the Persian King's top priority. His fundamental preoccupation in the early years of his reign was securing his throne and his family's hold on power after the assassination of his father (and perhaps brother) by close members of the royal household. This could be accomplished only with a resolute internal focus on ensuring the peace and security of his realm. So instead of plotting to invade Greece, the King returned to an age-old Persian policy of financially supporting others who wished to push back against the Greek alliance of the Delian League. In this he needed little from Themistocles, and Plutarch suggests that, as a result, Themistocles spent the rest of the 460s in relative calm in his new home in Magnesia.[22]

While living in Magnesia, Themistocles issued a series of silver coins with his own name on them – they are in fact the only surviving contemporary evidence of him from his entire lifetime. These coins are revealing of the way in which Themistocles once again struck a different course from those around him, as he had so often done throughout his life, and perhaps a little of how he viewed himself and the different influences on his life. Minting coins in this period was an expensive process, and usually it was undertaken only by a monarch, a tyrant ruler, or a city-state. Themistocles was technically the ruler of the cities given to him by the Persian King – but his rulership was in the King's name only. That he minted these coins thus underlines the way Themistocles sought, even late in his life and career, even after all his experiences, to push the boundaries of what was customary, particularly when it came to articulating the power and importance of his own position.

His desire to stand out is even more apparent when we look at the details (no doubt chosen by him) in the coins themselves. For a start, the coins were minted on the Attic standard in terms of their weight, which was unusual for the region and linked them directly back to Themistocles' long-term home of Athens. Second, Themistocles added his own name to his coins, an unusual decision for a ruler in the period before 450 BCE, and he did so in the Greek alphabet instead of Persian, again an unusual choice for the region. Both elements made him stand out in his new realm. At the same time, however, the main image on the obverse of most of the coins was that of Apollo – an image pertinent both to Greece and to the city of Magnesia, where Apollo had an important cult – connecting both the Greek and the Persian realm and making the coinage relevant to his new community. Here was an image of Themistocles as understanding and connecting his two cultures, while simultaneously underlining his Athenian heritage and his own sense of importance, and, as a result, indulging his lifelong trait of standing apart from the crowd.

On several other, smaller denomination coins issued by Themistocles, there is an image of a bearded man, with the first and last letters of Themistocles' name framing the head. Scholars have argued that this is meant to represent Themistocles himself—his own self-issued portrait on smaller coinage for local circulation at a time when it was still very unusual indeed for a local ruler to strike a coin with his own portrait. Perhaps he was testing the waters of what was possible, careful not to stray as far in his hubris as Demaratus had done and annoy the King. On the coins, Themistocles does not wear the normal attire of a Persian governor—or anything that might remotely resemble the tiara Demaratus sought, but instead a tight "beret" hat.[23] But if this is Themistocles, then the coin reminds us of the Themistocles of old in Athens, who found it impossible to resist putting the emphasis on himself rather than on the collective. It is a sign perhaps that, while he had learned many things during his long career, mastering his own need for attention—whatever the costs of it—was not his forte.

But Themistocles' late life was not entirely one of leisure, rulership, and coin minting—or without incident. He is said by Plutarch to have recognized in Sardis, in one of the temples, an object stolen from Athens by the Persians in 480 and to have tried to get it returned to Greece. The governor of the region was outraged at the suggestion and threatened to write to the King to report Themistocles' behavior, at which point Themistocles had to bring back into play his old skills of soothing ruffled feathers by roundabout ways (in this case by bribing the governor's concubines to plead his case).[24]

On another occasion he faced an assassination attempt by a group of Persians led by another provincial governor. Themistocles avoided the attack, thanks, it was claimed, to an intervention in a dream by the divine Anahita, the Persian incarnation of the "mother of the gods"; Themistocles later built a temple in Magnesia in her honor, assigning his own daughter to be the priestess (as the goddess had herself requested). It must have been clear to Themistocles that although his new life gamble had paid off in grand style, his position was not unchangeable, or indefinitely secure. He was no longer a plane tree rooted deep in the ground and just as insecure in the Persian landscape as he had been forced to realize he was in the Athenian landscape. As he entered his sixties, he was a man against whom the tide would, he knew, turn at some point – and turn in a way that even he could not escape.

That tide came in the form of Athenian assistance to a growing revolt from within the Persian King's own empire. In 460, a man who claimed descent from Egypt's ancient dynasties led a revolt against Persian rule in Egypt. In this he was actively supported by the Athenians, to whom he had reached out for help. An Athenian fleet of some two hundred triremes was at the time conducting a campaign against Cyprus – extending Athenian influence farther and farther down along the coast of Asia Minor into the Levant. The admiral, Charitimides, led the fleet, along with a good number of troops, to Egypt and sailed up the Nile. Joining with the leader of the Egyptian rebellion in late 460, they engaged the Persians at Papremis and secured victory over the numerically superior Persian forces. Their commander, the Persian satrap Achaemenes, a brother of the Persian King, was killed in the battle. The remaining Persians retreated along the Nile back to Memphis, pursued by the Athenians and Egyptians, who secured a further victory over the Persian fleet. While the final rump of the Persian army barricaded itself in the city of Memphis, the Athenians and Egyptians first underlined their victories by sending the body of the dead satrap back to his brother, and then settled in to lay siege to the remaining Persian troops in Memphis.

The Athenians, led on by Cimon, had now directly threatened the integrity of the Persian realm.[25] While Artaxerxes battled the

Egyptian and Athenian armies in Egypt (armies he would finally defeat in 454), he also began preparations for a Persian offensive against Greek – and particularly Athenian – power in the Aegean and ultimately in Greece itself. To this end, he called upon Themistocles to make good on his promises and help, with his expert knowledge of Greek affairs, plan the attack.

In 459, at the age of sixty-five, Themistocles had nowhere left to run, and was finally put in a position in which he had little choice but to support the King in an attack on Greece. Plutarch argues that partly because he did not think such an attack could ever be successful, and partly because he did not want to tarnish any further the memory of his own achievements, Themistocles decided to end his own life. After gathering friends and family and sacrificing to the gods, he drank bull's blood (or, in some sources, a different poison).[26] Taking one's own life was an honorable action in ancient Greek – and indeed Persian – culture; it was a tradition long embraced in myth, tragedy, and historical events. Suicide was seen as an honorable release from a life made undesirable by the insurmountable loss of honor and piling-on of shame. Indeed, the Persian King Artaxerxes, on hearing the news, is said not to have expressed anger or frustration that Themistocles had evaded making good on his promise but instead to have declared his admiration for Themistocles' decision and continued to treat his family with respect. In future decades, as more and more Greeks came to serve Persian Kings, it would become a regular claim that each Persian ruler would make to attract the most skilled to serve them: the newcomers would have more influence with them than even Themistocles had.[27]

Epilogue

Plutarch tells us that the Magnesians had a splendid tomb built in honor of Themistocles in their marketplace. But he also acknowledges that many stories circulated about what happened to Themistocles' remains: some reported that they were stolen by the Athenians and scattered disrespectfully about, or, alternatively, that a tomb in the shape of an altar was built on a promontory jutting out facing the Athenian harbor of Piraeus so that it could be viewed (and cheered) by sailors entering or exiting the harbor.[1] Thucydides, on the other hand, offers us a variant in which, following his own wishes, Themistocles' bones were brought back secretly to Athens by some of his friends and buried without a tomb, because of his formal status as a traitor.[2] The variety of stories reflects the diverse views on Themistocles at the time of his death in the early 450s: honored local elite ruler, disgraced condemned traitor, hero of Athenian sailors, outcast still beloved by some.

Yet this full spectrum of reactions would die away not long after his death, leaving behind a much narrower, and more positive, view of him and his achievements. For even as he was dying in Asia Minor in 459 BCE, the political wind in Athens was changing again. Cimon, no friend of Themistocles', who had been in the ascendancy in the late 470s and into the 460s, himself fell foul of the Athenian people and was ostracized in 460. At the same time, new democratic leaders, men like Pericles and Ephialtes, were launching political assaults on the final bastion of aristocratic power in Athens, the Areopagus, aimed at reducing its constitutional power. Thus, just as Themistocles' posthumous reputation was being crystallized, Athens became (and began to recognize itself as) a real system of people power – a demokratia – and began simultaneously to grow into the center of an empire. In 454, five years after Themistocles' death, the treasury of the Delian League, until that time situated on the island of Delos, was moved symbolically to Athens, and the inscribed Athenian tribute-quota lists – recording a fixed portion of the money paid to them by members of their empire – started to emerge. It was in this heady period of both people power and seaborne imperial power that Athens began to reconsider what Themistocles had achieved and what he stood for. Despite his status as a traitor condemned to death who had gone into the service of the Persian King, Themistocles' sons were formally welcomed back to Athens in the 450s, and we are told by the second-century CE travel guide Pausanias that even in his own day a painting of Themistocles, dedicated by Themistocles' sons, hung inside the Parthenon.[3] This was a phenomenal turnaround: a portrait of Themistocles as an individual, despite Athenians' previous revulsion at the idea of spotlighting the individual over the collective, formally dedicated inside the Parthenon. Nor was this just any temple in Athens. The Parthenon was the latest creation of the demokratia and had itself been paid for in part by the tribute extracted from Athens's new empire. It had quickly become the symbol of Athens's people power and imperial power. That a portrait of Themistocles was dedicated here in the decades after his death shows how quickly Themistocles had been rehabilitated.

In the ensuing context of Athenian supremacy and empire, due to its preeminent fleet, and its subsequent fight for survival during the Peloponnesian War in the second half of the fifth century BCE, Themistocles' actions (and successes) as a military leader, his association with the building up of the fleet itself, not to mention the protection of Athens with its vital city walls, became the keynotes of his story, rather than his ego, his ostracism, and his condemnation as a traitor.[4] The harking back to a period of military success became even more pronounced after Athens lost its empire at the end of the century and struggled to reestablish itself in the first half of the fourth century BCE. Courtroom and political orators like Lysias, Isocrates, and Demosthenes began to speak of a previous Golden Age of Athens, in which its leaders – including men like Themistocles – had been better than Athens's leaders of their own day.[5] In the mid-fourth century, when Athenian democracy felt more constantly under threat, Themistocles' status as a military leader of Athens's Golden Age took on a more starkly democratic sheen, and Themistocles was more often portrayed as one of the key proponents and deliverers of people power. There is no clearer symbol of Themistocles' rehabilitation from condemned traitor to democratic hero in Athens than the adoption at this time of his once-hated Temple of Artemis Aristoboule (complete with the portrait of himself), apparently as the central deme shrine of Melite. The temple was substantially refurbished in 330 BCE, continuing in use long afterward, perhaps, as some have argued, even in dual use as a sanctuary of Artemis and a hero shrine for Themistocles.[6] Such a crystallization of Themistocles' illustrious posthumous reputation at times both of military glory and of defeat for Athens helps us understand what later puzzled Cicero so much:

although Themistocles had served Athens brilliantly only once in battle (at Salamis), he was more famous than someone like Solon, who had created a new political system that served the city continuously.[7]

This posthumous image of Themistocles as a heroic and cunning military leader has encouraged scholars and others over the generations to forget his complex development as an individual, the intricacies of his career, and the incongruities of his reputation. What we have seen crucially in this biography of Themistocles is a man who was not simply blessed by nature to carry out the actions and occupy the roles for which he would later become famous and respected. Rather, he was a man whose character, abilities, and actions were nurtured and shaped by the things he experienced throughout his life. He was born into a period of tumultuous change and uncertainty for Athens, and he grew up as something of an outsider within his own society. As he came of age, his was a journey of development to master his character and actions; to understand how the changing political system could be navigated; and to learn what should be expected of those who sought to lead the city. In that journey he was as much at risk of falling foul of the Athenians as anyone else, and as often as he persuaded others to an action, he failed to persuade others to follow him, or had to recognize that his ideas had found no favor. Moreover, as quickly as he pushed himself to the center of Athenian affairs, so he was relinquished and cast aside. And although he often demonstrated a good sense of how to judge the political mood of a group or individuals, he too could make mistakes, ultimately mistakes that led to his ostracism and disgrace. This roller-coaster journey must have fed his sense of uncertainty about his status, his insecurity, and his constant search for individual fame, but it also gave him the abilities and resilience that made him a survivor, a man who was able to learn new ways of living within a very different world even in his final decade. For tenacity alone, he deserves our respect.

Finally, what should we make of Thucydides' claim that Themistocles was, along with the Spartan general Pausanius, the "most illustrious Greek of his time"? The word for "illustrious" in the Greek is *lampros.* It translates literally as "bright," "radiant," or "gleaming" when used of the sun, the moon, or weaponry reflecting the sun's rays. But it can also be translated as "distinct," "strong," "impressive," "unambiguous" in relation to natural forces, and as "dazzling," "magnificent," "splendid," "glorious," and "illustrious" in relation to people.

For Thucydides, as we saw at the beginning of this book, the title "illustrious" was merited thanks to Themistocles' "natural" talents – an assertion that in many ways I have sought to undermine by offering a portrait of a person in a constant process of evolution and development who succeeded and failed, and whose permanent reputation as illustrious was secured only due to societal developments after his death. As such, if we simply label him as "illustrious," "glorious," "dazzling," or "splendid," we at best miss the point and at worst are simply wrong. But in other ways, the term Thucydides used, "lampros," is without doubt appropriate for Themistocles. He was from the outset a "distinct," "strong" force. He achieved "impressive" things and could be resolute and "unambiguous" (as much as he also shape-shifted and reinvented himself). At moments, he was "radiant and" "gleaming," like a sword catching the sun, in his actions, his words, his plans, and his resilience and tenacity. He perhaps does merit the epithet "lampros," but not in the standard sense. Does he though, on the basis of this definition, deserve the title "most illustrious of his time"? As a strong, distinct, tenacious force, he does. He was never the plane tree he thought he was, but he was certainly more than a ship that could be left aside to rot.

What such a title – merited or not – still obscures, as I think Themistocles' story as I have told it here makes clear, are two key points. First, no one achieves great things on his (or her) own. As Cicero himself would later emphasize in his own studies of statesmanship, Themistocles would never have accomplished even his most infamous successes without the support of other key individuals around him: whether it was Cimon who supported the plan to evacuate Athens; Mnesiphilus who helped shape the scheme to keep the fleet at Salamis; or Aristides who helped convince the council of commanders to fight at Salamis.[8] Without taking away from Themistocles' talent, energy, resilience, and determination – or his need for fame and glory – it is only in the context of the actions and support of others that his deeds became worthy of being described as "lampros."

Second, as we have seen time and again in the writing of history, it is easier and often more forceful, when writing about the past, to hang extremes of behavior and achievement, as exempla for the future, around individuals rather than groups. Plutarch recounts that Themistocles was once asked, while attending the Olympic Games, whether he would rather be Achilles or Homer. He is said to have queried with incredulity why anyone would not choose to be an Olympic victor over the crier who proclaimed the victor.[9] For him the choice was simple: Achilles the doer, not Homer the teller. But as we have seen in this examination of Themistocles' own life and in the development of his posthumous reputation, individual history tellers and societies as a whole, as part of their own processes of evolution and recollection, shape the long-term images of heroes, and it is to them, ultimately, that Themistocles' owes his elevated position in Greek affairs. Perhaps if Themistocles were given the choice again with the benefit of historical hindsight, he might opt for Homer over Achilles.

Chronology

All dates BCE.

546/5	Seizure of power in Athens by Peisistratus
527	Death of Peisistratus, turannos leader of Athens; Hippias, son of Peisistratus, becomes turannos
525/4	Cleisthenes, of the Alcmaeonid family, elected chief archon of Athens
524/3	Birth of Themistocles Miltiades, of the Philaid family, elected chief archon of Athens
522/1	Peisistratus, grandson of the turannos Peisistratus, elected chief archon of Athens
514	Murder of Hipparchus, brother of Hippias, at the Panathenaia in Athens
511	Spartan army lands at Phaleron, the port of Athens, to help expel Hippias
510	Spartan army returns in a second (successful) attempt to expel Hippias
508/7	Isagoras elected chief archon of Athens Cleisthenes proposes his plans for change to the Athenian political system Spartan army called in by Isagoras to help expel Cleisthenes and his supporters; Cleisthenes goes into exile The Athenian demos rise up in revolt against Isagoras's imposed system of government and Spartan intervention, leading to the expulsion of Isagoras and his Spartan supporters Cleisthenes returns to Athens and his plans for reform are adopted
506	The Spartan king, with Boeotian and Chalcidian support, leads an attack on Athens to reinstall Isagoras; defeated by Athenian troops
505	Aegina attacks Phaleron
ca. 504–490	Sometime in this period Themistocles probably married his first wife
499	Beginning of the Ionian Revolt against the Persian King, led by Aristagoras; Athens sends ships to support the revolt and the burning of Sardis Miltiades sets out to capture the islands of Lemnos and Imbros
494/3	The Persians put an end to the Ionian Revolt

Chronology

493/2	Themistocles elected chief archon of Athens Miltiades returns to Athens; is put on trial for having acted as turannos in the Chersonesus and acquitted Phrynichus puts on a play about the sack of Miletus at the City Dionysia in Athens Athens decides to develop a new, larger port at Piraeus
492	The Persian army and navy begin an advance toward Greece, but suffer multiple setbacks
490	The Persian navy sets sail again across the Aegean to attack Eretria and Athens The Persians land at Marathon in Attica, with Hippias in their ranks; Themistocles and Aristides fight at the Battle of Marathon; the Persian army is forced to flee
490/89	Miltiades leads expedition to Paros, which fails Miltiades is put on trial in Athens; dies
489/8	Aristides elected chief archon of Athens
488/7	First use of ostracism at Athens; Hipparchus, a member of the Peisistratid family, exiled
487/6	Ostracism of Megacles, of the Alcmaeonid family Introduction of comedy to the City Dionysia Reform to the system of electing the chief archon of Athens
485	Xerxes becomes ruler of Persia following death of his father, Darius
484/3	Ostracism of Xanthippus
483/2	Discovery of a new seam of silver at Laurium; the Athenians vote to use the silver to build a fleet Beginning of Persian preparations to invade Greece
482/1	Ostracism of Aristides
480	Spring: Greek allies head north to Tempe to face the Persians but quickly return June–July: Persian navy and army move along the north Aegean coast and begin to descend toward central Greece August: Battles of Thermopylae (on land) and Artemisium (at sea) Early September: the Athenians evacuate Athens September 23: the Persians sack and burn the city of Athens September 24: Themistocles sends his slave to Xerxes to encourage the Persian King to encircle and engage the Greek fleet at Salamis September 25: Battle of Salamis; Persian fleet is defeated and starts to sail back to the Hellespont

Chronology

479	Battle of Plataea Battle of Mycale
478	Siege of Sestus by Xanthippus Delian League formed Rebuilding of Athens's city walls begins with Themistocles' leadership; expansion of Athenian fleet and port facilities begins; Themistocles' embassy to Sparta to enable the Athenians to finish building their city walls
477	Aristides asked to conduct the first assessment of tribute for the Delian League
476/5	Construction of the Theseion in Athens
ca. 475	Construction of the Temple of Artemis Aristoboule by Themistocles in the deme of Melite in Athens
472	Performance of Aeschylus's *Persians* at the City Dionysia
ca. 471	Ostracism of Themistocles
ca. 468	Athenians sent to arrest Themistocles in Argos and bring him to Athens to face trial for treason; Themistocles flees to northern Greece
468–465	Themistocles makes his way from northern Greece to the west coast of Asia, starts to travel to the court of the Persian King
466	Athenians defeat the Persian fleet at the Battle of Eurymedon
ca. 465	Themistocles meets with the Persian King to ask for sanctuary and offer his services
465	Artaxerxes becomes ruler of the Persians, following the death of Xerxes
ca. 465–460	Themistocles installed as favorite of the Persian King, is given Magnesia to rule
460	Athens provides assistance to a revolt in Egypt against Persian rule Ostracism of Cimon
459	Themistocles called upon by Artaxerxes to help with planning of new campaign against Athens Death of Themistocles
454	Treasury of the Delian League moved from Delos to Athens

Notes

All translations are mine unless otherwise indicated. Classical sources are cited by internal divisions so that any translation may be used; most can be accessed online via the Perseus database or the web-based Loeb Classical Library; other recommended translations are cited in the list of abbreviations.

ABBREVIATIONS

Ael. *VH*	Aelianus, *Various Histories* [*Varia Historia*]
Arist. [*Ath. Pol.*]	Aristotle, *The Constitution of the Athenians* [*Athenaion Politeiai*]
Cic.	Cicero
Diod. Sic.	Diodorus Siculus, *Historical Library* [*Bibliotheca Historica*]
Hdt.	Herodotus, *The Histories* (*Herodotus: The Histories*, trans. Tom Holland [London: Penguin, 2013])
Nep. *Them.*	Cornelius Nepos, *Themistocles* (*Cornelius Nepos: Lives of the Great Commanders*, Trans. Quintus Curtius [Charleston, S.C.: Fortress of the Mind, 2019])
Paus.	Pausanias, *Description of Greece* [*Hellados Periegesis*]
Plut.	Plutarch
Mor.	*Morals* [*Moralia*]
Vit. Arist.	Life of Aristides
Vit. Cim.	Life of Cimon
Vit. Them.	Life of Themistocles (*Life of Themistocles*, 2nd ed., ed. and trans. J. L. Marr [Oxford: Aris and Philips, 2015])
Polyaenus, *Strat.*	Polyaenus, *Stratagems* [*Strategemata*] (*Stratagems of War*, trans. Peter Krentz and Everett L. Wheeler [London: Ares, 1994])
Thuc.	Thucydides, *The Peloponnesian War* (*Thucydides: The War of the Peloponnesians and the Athenians*, ed. and trans. Jeremy Mynott [Cambridge: Cambridge University Press, 2013])
Xen. *Mem.*	Xenophon, *Memorabilia*

PROLOGUE

1. Plut. *Vit. Them.* 15.3.

2. Thuc. 1.138. See also Diod. Sic. 11.23.3: Pausanias and Themistocles were "the most distinguished leaders of the Greeks." See also Nep. *Them.* 5: "Thus through

the cleverness of one man the liberty of Greece was assured and Asia succumbed to Europe."

3. Thuc. 1.138.3. See also Plut. *Mor.* 343a; *Vit. Cim.* 5.1; Cic., *On oratory* 2.299–300, 3.59; Diod. Sic. 11.58.5. See also Xenophon (*Mem.* 4.2.2), who wondered whether it was "constant intercourse with some wise man or by natural ability" that Themistocles stood out as a leader to the Athenians in times of need.

4. Martin Robertson *A History of Greek Art*, vol. 1 (Cambridge: Cambridge University Press, 1975), 187, 504; Anthony J. Podlecki, *The Life of Themistocles: A Critical Survey of the Literary and Archaeological Evidence* (Montreal: McGill-Queens University Press, 1975), 143–146 (likeness taken from images set up in his honor in Athens or Magnesia); Brunilde Ridgeway *The Severe Style in Greek Sculpture* (Princeton: Princeton University Press, 1970), 99 (created during his lifetime).

CHAPTER 1. AMBIGUOUS BEGINNINGS

1. Plut. *Vit. Them.* 1.1; Hdt. 7.143. For discussion of the year see John K. Davies, *Athenian Propertied Families, 600–300 BCE* (Oxford: Clarendon, 1971), 214–215. The ancient deme of Phrearrhioi is in the region of the modern village of Pheriza/Feriza in Greece.

2. Plut. *Vit. Them.* 1; Nep. *Them.* 1.

3. Athenaeus, *Deipnosophistae* 13.37. Aelian also recounts that Themistocles' mother was Abrotonon (*VH* 12.43). See also Plut. *Vit. Them.* 1. To this needs to be added Nep. *Them.* 1 (whose text, depending on how you interpret the manuscript, has Themistocles' mother coming either from the deme of Acharnai in Attica, or alternatively from Akarnania in northwestern Greece).

4. See Hdt. 5.94; Robin Osborne, "Law, the Democratic Citizen and the Representation of Women in Classical Athens," in *Athens and Athenian Democracy*. ed. Osborne (Cambridge: Cambridge University Press, 2010), 244–266. For wider discussion of the changing definition of a nothos within Athenian society see Deborah Kamen, *Status in Classical Athens* (Princeton: Princeton University Press, 2013), 62–70.

5. See Peter Bicknell, "Themistokles' Father and Mother," *Historia* 31, no. 2 (1982): 161–173.

6. Plato, [*Hipparchus*] 228b–229c; Arist. [*Ath. Pol.*] 18.1.

7. Plato, *Protagoras* 326a.

8. Plut. *Vit. Them.* 2.1–5.

9. Libanius, *Declamations* 9 and 10.

10. Arist. [*Ath. Pol.*] 13–19; see also Plut. *Vit. Sol.* 13; Hdt. 1.59–64.

CHAPTER 2. A WORLD IN CRISIS

1. Arist. [*Ath. Pol.*] 19.1 (wise fellow); Hdt 5.62; Thuc. 6.59.2.

2. Hdt. 5.62.

3. Hdt. 5.66 (added the *demos*), 5.69.2. Cf. Hdt. 5.63.1, 5.90; Arist. [*Ath. Pol.*] 20.1.

4. See Antony Andrewes, "Kleisthenes' Reform Bill," *Classical Quarterly* 27 (1977): 241–248; David M. Lewis, "Cleisthenes and Attica," *Historia* 12, no. 1 (1963): 22–40.

5. Hdt. 5.72.

6. Hdt. 5.74.

7. See Hdt. 5.73–77; Charles W. Fornara, ed., *Archaic Times to the End of the Peloponnesian War*, 2nd ed. (Baltimore: Johns Hopkins University Press, 1983), 43–44.

CHAPTER 3. TIPPING POINTS

1. See Plut. *Vit. Them.* 22.2; Anthony J. Podlecki, *The Life of Themistocles: A Critical Survey of the Literary and Archaeological Evidence* (Montreal: McGill-Queens University Press, 1975), 3.

2. Plut. *Vit. Them.* 1.2. Ancient writers often suggested Themistocles had to endure disdain because of his low birth: see, e.g., Life of Sophocles 1.

3. Plut. *Vit. Them.* 3.2.

4. Plut. *Vit. Them.* 2.6–7.

5. Plut. *Vit. Them.* 2.7; Nep. *Them.* 1. Veracity of this claim discussed in Plut. *Vit. Them.* 2.8; Libanius, *Declamations* 9.8, 9.11, 9.13, 9.21–22, 9.29.

6. Libanius, *Declamations* 10.4–5, 10.7, 10.9.

7. Plut. *Vit. Them.* 2.7.

8. Plut. *Vit. Them.* 2.7; see Ael. *VH* 2.12; Plut. *Mor.* 800b; Cornelius Nepos, *Aristides* 1.

9. See Plut. *Vit. Them.* 3.1–2; *Vit. Arist.* 2.

10. For the Ionian Revolt see Hdt. 5.97. For Miltiades' return to Athens: David Stuttard, *Phoenix: A Father, a Son, and the Rise of Athens* (Cambridge: Harvard University Press, 2021), 55–63. For Themistocles' archonship: Dion. Hal. *Ant. Rom.* 6.34.1; Charles Fornara, "Themistocles' Archonship," *Historia* 20, nos. 5–6 (1971): 534–540; Robert J. Lenardon, "The Archonship of Themistocles, 493/2," *Historia* 5, no. 4 (1956): 401–419; Alden A. Mosshammer, "Themistocles' Archonship in the Chronographic Tradition," *Hermes* 103, no. 2 (1975): 222–234.

CHAPTER 4. CALLING THE SHOTS

1. For the play see Hdt. 6.21, and for the trial see Hdt. 6.104.

2. Plut. *Vit. Them.* 31, 32.

3. Hdt. 5.105.

4. Miltiades: Hdt. 6.104.

5. Thuc. 1.93.3. Cf. Eusebius, *Chronicle* (Olympiad 71.1). A good English translation is available via the Attalus digital project: https://www.attalus.org/translate/

eusebius.html. For discussion: Charles Fornara, "Themistocles' Archonship," *Historia* 20, nos. 5–6 (1971): 534–540; Alden A. Mosshammer, "Themistocles' Archonship in the Chronographic Tradition," *Hermes* 103, no. 2 (1975): 222–234; Anthony J. Podlecki, *The Life of Themistocles: A Critical Survey of the Literary and Archaeological Evidence* (Montreal: McGill-Queens University Press, 1975), 7.

6. See Hdt. 7.133; Paus. 3.12.7; Plut. *Vit. Them.* 6.2; Aelius Aristides, *Orations* 3.184, 1.99.

7. Hdt. 6.44–45.

8. Plato, *Menexenus,* 240b.

9. See Peter Krentz, *The Battle of Marathon* (New Haven: Yale University Press, 2010), 90–94.

10. Hdt. 6.101.

11. Hdt. 6.101–109. For discussion of the different views of modern scholars, see David Stuttard, *Phoenix: A Father, a Son, and the Rise of Athens* (Cambridge: Harvard University Press, 2021), 82.

12. For their position in the line see Plut. *Vit. Arist.* 5.3–7. For the agreement see Polyaenus, *Strat.* 1.31.1; Plut. *Vit. Arist.* 5.4; Justinus, *Epitome* 2.9.15. For discussion of whether this agreement took place at Marathon or before the later Battle of Salamis see Podlecki, *The Life of Themistocles,* 8.

13. Hdt. 6.112; Aristophanes, *The Wasps* 1081.

14. Aristophanes, *The Knights* 781.

15. On the fighting see Plut. *Vit. Arist.* 5.3–7; on the Persian retreat, see Hdt. 6.113.

16. Hdt. 6.116; Plut. *Vit. Arist.* 5.5.

17. Paus. 1.32.3.

CHAPTER 5. THE POWER OF EXCLUSION

1. Plut. *Vit. Them.* 3.4.

2. Plut. *Vit. Cim.* 8.1; see also Charles W. Fornara, ed., *Archaic Times to the End of the Peloponnesian War,* 2nd ed. (Baltimore: Johns Hopkins University Press, 1983), 49.

3. Fornara, *Archaic Times to the End of the Peloponnesian War,* 49–50; see also Michael Scott, *Delphi and Olympia: The Spatial Politics of Panhellenism in the Archaic and Classical Periods* (Cambridge: Cambridge University Press, 2010), 77–80.

4. Plut. *Vit. Them.* 3.4.

5. Hdt. 6.136.

6. See Cornelius Nepos, *Cimon* 1–4.

7. Arist. [*Ath. Pol.*] 22.

8. Hdt. 6.115; Arist. [*Ath. Pol.*] 22.1–5. See also Harold Mattingly, "The Practice of Ostracism at Athens," *Antichthon* 25 (1991): 1–26; Sara Forsdyke, *Exile, Ostracism, and Democracy: The Politics of Expulsion in Ancient Greece* (Princeton: Princeton University Press, 2005), 155–156; cf. Philochoros in F. Jacoby, *Fragmente der griechischen Historiker* (Berlin: Weidmann, 1923–1959), F30.

9. Pindar, *Pythian Odes* 7.

10. See Arist. [*Ath. Pol.*] 22.5; Robert J. Buck, "The Reforms of 487 BC in the Selection of Archons," *Classical Philology* 60, no. 2 (1965): 96–101. For discussion on potential roles Themistocles played in this change see Anthony J. Podlecki, *The Life of Themistocles: A Critical Survey of the Literary and Archaeological Evidence* (Montreal: McGill-Queens University Press, 1975), 10.

11. Arist. [*Ath. Pol.*] 22.

12. Arist. [*Ath. Pol.*] 22.

13. See Manuel Regueiro, Michael Stamatakis, and Konstantinos Laskaridis, "The Geology of the Acropolis (Athens, Greece)," *European Geologist* 38 (2014): 45–52; Panos Valavanis, "The Acropolis," in *The Cambridge Companion to Ancient Athens*, ed. Jenifer Neils and Dylan K. Rogers (Cambridge: Cambridge University Press, 2021), 66.

14. On Themistocles as a manipulator of the system see David Stuttard, *Phoenix: A Father, a Son, and the Rise of Athens* (Cambridge: Harvard University Press, 2021), 101; Jeffrey A. Smith, *Themistocles: The Powerbroker of Athens* (London: Pen and Sword, 2021), 46; Peter Green, *The Graeco-Persian Wars* (Berkeley: University of California Press, 1998), 59. On Themistocles as a creator of the system see the discussion in Forsdyke, *Exile, Ostracism, and Democracy*, 282.

15. Arist. [*Ath. Pol.*] 22.

16. For discussion of the possible political "duo" of Themistocles and Mnesiphilus see Frank J. Frost, "Themistocles and Mnesiphilus," *Historia* 20, no. 1 (1971): 20–25. In total, thousands of ostraca have been found bearing Themistocles' name. In particular a cache of ostraca was found in the Agora, thought to date from the 480s, with 191 ostraca bearing Themistocles' name as the preferred candidate for ostracism, but written in only fourteen different hands. Was this a case of ostraca being officially prepared for use by those who could not write themselves, or perhaps an attempt to cheat the system? See Robin Osborne, *Greece in the Making, 1200–479 BC*, 2nd ed. (London: Routledge, 2009), 332. For dating of this cache instead to an ostracism vote in 471 BCE, see Mattingly, "The Practice of Ostracism at Athens."

17. See Mattingly, "The Practice of Ostracism at Athens." One of the ostraca declaring a vote for Xanthippus was inscribed, "This ostracon says that Xanthippus, son of Arriphron, has done the most harm of all the cursed leaders": Russell Meiggs and David Lewis, eds., *A Selection of Greek Historical Inscriptions to the End of the Fifth Century BC*, 2nd ed. (Oxford: Clarendon, 1988), 42.

CHAPTER 6. TURNING TO THE SEA

1. Thuc. (6.97.7) described "more than twenty thousand" slaves who absconded to join the Spartans in the late fifth century BCE. See John Kroll, "Coinage and Its Economic Implications," in *The Cambridge Companion to Ancient Athens*, ed. Jenifer Neils and Dylan K. Rogers (Cambridge: Cambridge University Press, 2021): 257–258. The area had a bad reputation for unhealthiness because of the toxic ash and fumes in the air: Xen. *Mem.* 3.6.

2. I have visited and crawled through the still surviving tunnels of the silver mines at Laurion. When you are inside, you immediately lose all sense of direction and time. The air is hot and stifling, with the dust that comes simply from people moving through (not even hacking at the rock) almost overwhelming. The tunnels move left, right, straight up, and straight down, following the long-extracted silver wherever it traveled, and you quickly feel as if the world has forgotten your existence.

3. Hdt. 7.144.

4. Hdt. 7.144; Plut. *Vit. Them.* 4; Arist. [*Ath. Pol.*] 22.7.

5. Hdt. 7.22–24. Later historians, such as Thucydides (4.109) mention the canal, and archaeological investigation has confirmed that it was built.

6. Plut. *Vit. Them.* 4.2.

7. Hdt. 6.87–93.

8. Plut. *Vit. Them.* 4.2. Diod. Sic (11.43.3) claims that Themistocles simultaneously chose to remove the tax on artisans and metics, to encourage great crowds of people to come to Athens and give the city the labor required for many crafts more easily.

9. Plut. *Vit. Them.* 3.4 (oiled). Cic., *Letters to Atticus* 10.8.4, describes Themistocles as the man who knew that mastery of the sea led to mastery of the empire. Hdt. 7.144 (never used for original purpose).

10. Plut. *Vit. Arist.* 7.1–4. See also Plut. *Vit. Them.* 5.6; Arist. [*Ath. Pol.*] 22.7.

11. See Sara Forsdyke, *Exile, Ostracism, and Democracy: The Politics of Expulsion in Ancient Greece* (Princeton: Princeton University Press, 2005), 157n63; Paul Cartledge, *Democracy: A Life,* 2nd ed. (Oxford: Oxford University Press, 2018), 71; on Aristides' ostracism see Plut. *Vit. Arist.* 7.6. On the triremes, see Hdt. 7.144. On Aristides' exile, see Arist. [*Ath. Pol.*] 22.8. The doubling of ships after the ostracism is discussed in Tom Holland, *Persian Fire* (London: Abacus, 2005) 221–222.

12. Hdt. 7.146.

13. Hdt. 7.140–142.

14. Hdt. 7.142.

15. Hdt 7.143; see also Nep. *Them.* 2.

16. Plut. *Vit. Them.* 6.1.

17. Plut. *Vit. Them.* 7.1.

18. Hdt. 7.56.

CHAPTER 7. FACING DESTRUCTION

1. Plut. *Vit. Them.* 7.1.

2. Hdt. 8.2–3; Plut. *Vit. Them.* 7.3.

3. Hdt. 7.201–210. A number of Greek cities, including Sparta, had sent only small detachments as advance guards to Thermopylae because the timing conflicted with two key religious festivals: for the Spartans, the Carneia, and for the rest of the (non-Dorian) Greeks, the Olympics. All the advance guard contingents promised that as soon as the festivals were over, every available man from their cities would be sent

to swell the Greek forces. Barry Strauss has calculated that the Olympics and the Carneia both ended with the full moon on August 19, 480: see Barry Strauss, *The Battle of Salamis: The Naval Encounter That Saved Greece – and Western Civilisation* (London: Simon and Schuster, 2004), xiii.

4. See Hdt 8.4–5; Plut. *Vit. Them.* 7.5; Richard Stoneman, *Xerxes: A Persian Life* (New Haven: Yale University Press, 2015), 136–138.

5. See Plut. *Vit. Them.* 7.6–7.

6. See Hdt. 8.41–42, 7.212–222, 238; Plut. *Vit. Them.* 8.2, 9.1–2; Justinus, *Epitome* 2.12.

7. Hdt. 8.11.

8. Hdt. 8.19.

9. Plut. *Vit. Them.* 8.1–2 (quoting Pindar).

10. Plut. *Vit. Them.* 9.1; Hdt. 8.22.

11. Hdt. 8.41; Plut. *Vit. Them.* 10. On Themistocles' proposal to abandon Athens see Arist. [*Ath. Pol.*] 22.7–23.1. For Themistocles' and Aristides' formal public putting aside of their enmity see Polyaenus, *Strat.* 1.31.1. For the cache of money to pay the triremes: Plut. *Vit. Them.* 10.1–8; 11.1; Arist. [*Ath. Pol.*] 23 suggests that it was actually the Areopagus that offered the required funds to encourage everyone to man the ships – and that, as a result of this, the Areopagus enjoyed a revived power and reverence in Athens after the victory at Salamis. See also Denver Graninger, "Plutarch on the Evacuation of Athens (*Themistocles* 10.8–9)," *Hermes* 138, no. 3 (2010): 308–317.

12. On the decree and the debate surrounding it, see Charles Fornara, ed., *Archaic Times to the End of the Peloponnesian War,* 2nd ed. (Baltimore: Johns Hopkins University Press, 1983), 53–54 (No. 55); Russell Meiggs and David Lewis, eds., *A Selection of Greek Historical Inscriptions to the End of the Fifth Century BC,* 2nd ed. (Oxford: Clarendon, 1988), 48–51 (No. 23); Michael H. Jameson, "A Decree of Themistocles from Troizen," *Hesperia* 29 (1960): 198–223; Noel Robertson, "The Decree of Themistocles in Its Contemporary Setting," *Phoenix* 36 (1982): 1–44; Mikael Johansson, "Plutarch, Aelius Aristides, and the Inscription from Troizen," *Rheinisches Museum für Philologie* 147 (2004): 343–353; Anthony J. Podlecki, *The Life of Themistocles: A Critical Survey of the Literary and Archaeological Evidence* (Montreal: McGill-Queens University Press, 1975), 147–167.

13. Hdt. 8.42–50.

14. On the Athenian decision to fight and the defense of the Acropolis see Plut. *Vit. Cim.* 5; Hdt. 8.49; Paus. 1.18.2; Strauss, *The Battle of Salamis,* xiii.

15. On the looting of Athens see Hdt. 8.51–53; Stoneman *Xerxes,* 139–142, including the way in which the burning of Athens was direct retribution for the burning of a temple in Sardis in 498 BCE and Xerxes' actions the following day to allow the Athenians with him to make sacrifices on the Acropolis to their own gods.

16. See Photius, *Bibliotheca* 72.23. For a translation, see *The Bibliotheca: A Selection,* trans. Nigel Guy Wilson (London: Duckworth, 2002).

17. Hdt. 8.59; Plut. *Vit. Them.* 11.2. See also Thuc. 1.74. For the following discussion see Diod. Sic. 11.15.4; Polyaenus, *Strat.* 1.30.1–7.

18. Hdt. 8.61; Plut. *Vit. Them.* 11.4–5. For discussion of the numbers of ships see Strauss, *The Battle of Salamis,* 79–80.

CHAPTER 8. THE HERO RISES—AND FALLS

1. Plut. *Vit. Them.* 12.1.

2. Plut. *Vit. Them.* 12.4–5 (quoting Aeschylus, *Persians* 355–360); Hdt. 8.75–76; see also Diod. Sic. 11.17.1; Nep. *Them.* 4.

3. Hdt. 8.79–82; Plut. *Vit. Them.* 12.6–8; Plut. *Vit. Aris.* 8.1–6.

4. Themistocles' speech: A. John Graham, "Themistocles' Speech Before Salamis: The Interpretation of Herodotus 8.83.1," *Classical Quarterly* 46, no. 2 (1996): 321–326; Vasiliki Zali, "Themistocles' Exhortation Before Salamis: On Herodotus 8.83," *Greek, Roman, and Byzantine Studies* 53 (2013): 461–485. See also Ael. *VH* 2.28, which claims that Themistocles included the example of a cockfight in his speech, leading to a later Athenian law in which, one day each year, a cockfight would take place in the theater. The sacrifice: Plut. *Vit. Them.* 13.2.

5. Plut. *Vit. Them.* 14.3; Hdt. 8.84–86.

6. Plut. *Vit. Them.* 17; see also Hdt. 8.123–124.

7. For events, see Hdt. 8.97–112; Plut. *Vit. Them.* 16; Justinus, *Epitome* 2.13.

8. Hdt. 8.109.

9. Hdt. 8.111.

10. See Didier Laroche and Anne Jacquemin, "Une base pour l'Apollon de Salamine à Delphes," *Bulletin de Correspondance Hellénique* 112 (1988): 235–246.

11. See Michael Scott, *Delphi and Olympia: The Spatial Politics of Panhellenism in the Archaic and Classical Periods* (Cambridge: Cambridge University Press, 2010), 84–85.

12. Hdt 7.139.

13. Hdt 8.125; Thuc. 1.74. Lysias (2.42), writing in the early fourth century BCE, suggested that the Athenians' supremacy at Salamis was due to three things: Themistocles' actions; having men with the most experience; and having more ships than any other of the allies. Demosthenes, writing in the later fourth century BCE, described how people used to think of the battle as the Athenians' fight, rather than Themistocles', in comparison to the prominence of individuals in his own day: Demosthenes 13.21–22 ("On Organization"). For Isocrates, also writing in the fourth century BCE, Themistocles should be, and was, "by the common assent of all" accredited with being responsible for the victory: Isocrates 12.51 ("Panathenaicus").

14. Ael. *VH* 13.43 records that this attention was what Themistocles was most proud of in his life.

15. Plut. *Vit. Arist.* 24.4.

CHAPTER 9. THE HERO RISES—AND FALLS (AGAIN)

1. Lycurgus 80–81 ("Against Leocrates"); Diod. Sic. 11.29.3.

2. Thuc. 1.91.

3. Thuc. 93.2; see also Leda Costaki and Anna Maria Theocharaki, "City Streets, Walls, and Gates," in *The Cambridge Companion to Ancient Athens,* ed. Jenifer Neils and Dylan K. Rogers (Cambridge: Cambridge University Press, 2021), 47–62; Anna Maria Theocharaki, "The Ancient Circuit Wall of Athens: Its Changing Course and the Phases of Construction," *Hesperia* 80, no. 1 (2011): 71–156.

4. Plut. *Vit. Them.* 19.1.

5. See Bjørn Lovén, *The Ancient Harbours of the Piraeus: The Zea Shipsheds and Slipways* (Athens: Danish Institute at Athens, 2011); George Steinhauer, "Piraeus: Harbours, Navy, and Shipping," in *The Cambridge Companion to Ancient Athens,* 231–243.

6. See Paul Cartledge, *Democracy: A Life,* 2nd ed. (Oxford: Oxford University Press, 2018), 74. By 463 BCE, "democracy" was definitely a recognized political concept, mentioned by that name in Aeschylus's *Suppliants* (line 604), performed that year.

7. Plut. *Vit Them.* 19.4–6.

8. Thuc. 1.90.

9. For events: Diod. Sic. 11.39.4, 11.40.1–4; Nep. *Them.* 7; Plut. *Vit. Them.* 19.1–2, 20.1–3; Thuc. 1.91–92. Xenophon (*Mem.* 2.6.13) records that Themistocles made the city love him by hanging an amulet around it (protecting it with walls). See also Aristophanes, *The Knights* 810–819, and Simon Hornblower, *The Greek World, 479–323 BC,* 4th ed. (London: Methuen, 2011), 33.

10. See Plut. *Vit. Cim.* 16.2. Plutarch also argues that Aristides encouraged the people of Athens to see Cimon as a more solid and reliable counter to Themistocles' daring: Plut. *Vit. Cim.* 5.6. See also Anthony J. Podlecki, *The Life of Themistocles: A Critical Survey of the Literary and Archaeological Evidence* (Montreal: McGill-Queens University Press, 1975), 35.

11. Plut. *Vit. Them.* 18.4.

12. Plut. *Vit. Them.* 5.4; Frank J. Frost, "Themistocles' Place in Athenian Politics," *California Studies in Classical Antiquity* 1 (1968): 105–124; Plut. *Mor.* 812a–c.

13. Although he lived in Melite and grew up in the deme of Phrearrhioi in southern Attica, in this period Demosthenes is thought to have reconstructed and redecorated the initiation shrine of the *genos* (clan) of the Lycomidai, which lay in the deme of Phyla in the northeast of Athens. He did this at his own expense as part of a claim that his family was connected to this noble ancient clan: Plut. *Vit Them.* 1.4; Podlecki *The Life of Themistocles,* 36.

14. On the shrine see Plut. *Vit. Them.* 22.2; *Mor.* 869c–d; John Travlos, *Pictorial Dictionary of Ancient Athens* (London: Thames and Hudson, 1971), 121; John M. Camp, *The Archaeology of Athens* (New Haven: Yale University Press, 2001),

61; Richard E. Wycherley, *The Stones of Athens* (Princeton: Princeton University Press, 1978), 189–190; Podlecki, *The Life of Themistocles*, 174–175.

15. The play highlights Themistocles' ruse to convince the Persian King to attack at Salamis, although it does not mention him by name: Aeschylus, *The Persians* 355. See Paul Cartledge, *Ancient Greek Political Thought in Practice* (Cambridge: Cambridge University Press, 2009), 65–66; Cartledge, *Democracy*, 83. Nor was this the only piece of contemporary literature praising Themistocles at the time; the (now mainly lost) poetry of Simonides also seems to have underlined Themistocles' contribution: see Podlecki, *The Life of Themistocles*, 48–51.

16. Plut. *Vit. Them.* 22; see also Plato, *Gorgias* 516d; Diod. Sic. 11.55.1; Demosthenes 23.205 ("Against Aristocrates"). One voter is said to have charged the archon who sponsored Aeschylus's *Persians* with abuse of his official position (perhaps because of his heroizing of Themistocles). One of the surviving ostraka from the vote of 471 BCE names Themistocles and adds, ironically, "to do him honor" (others are less polite and record insults against him): see Sara Forsdyke, *Exile, Ostracism, and Democracy: The Politics of Expulsion in Ancient Greece* (Princeton: Princeton University Press, 2005), 155; Harold Mattingly, "The Practice of Ostracism at Athens," *Antichthon* 25 (1991): 1–26. The Hellenistic writer Idomeneus of Lampsacus tells a tale recorded nowhere else of Themistocles' even going so far as to ride around the Agora in a chariot either with, or harnessed to, four prostitutes (F. Jacoby, *Fragmente der griechischen Historiker* [Berlin: Weidmann, 1923–1959], F4); Alex Gottesman *Politics and the Street in Democratic Athens* (Cambridge: Cambridge University Press, 2014), 14.

17. Plutarch, Life of Cato the Elder 8.3; Anon., *Letters of Themistocles* 4.15. For discussion about the usefulness of the *Letters of Themistocles*, dated to the first to second century CE, as source material see Podlecki, *The Life of Themistocles*, 129–134.

18. Nearly two thousand ostraka have been found with Themistocles' name on them. The next highest number of ostraka found for another individual is a little over two hundred. It is to this ostracism that the cache of ostraca with Themistocles' name on written in fourteen hands has been dated (as perhaps part of the campaign against him). It was perhaps not only Themistocles' enemies engaging in this practice—a cache of ostraka prepared again in the same hand has also been found for another Athenian, Kallixenos (comprising 15 percent of the surviving votes for his ostracism): Mattingly, "The Practice of Ostracism at Athens." See also Cartledge, *Ancient Greek Political Thought in Practice*, 65–66; Podlecki, *The Life of Themistocles*, 185–194.

CHAPTER 10. REINVENTION

1. Thuc. 1.128–134; Diod. Sic. 11.54.3–5, 11.55.3–5, 11.55.7–8.

2. For Themistocles' actions see Plut. *Vit. Them.* 23; Thuc. 1.135; for a wider discussion of the relationship between Themistocles and Pausanias, Anthony J. Podlecki, "Themistocles and Pausanias," *Rivista di Filologia e di Istruzione Classica* 104 (1976): 293–311; for Themistocles in exile, W. George Forrest, "Themistocles and Argos,"

Classical Quarterly 10 (1960): 233–234. One of the later anonymous *Letters of Themistocles* (2) is set during Themistocles' time in Argos; he writes to the Spartan Pausanias to explain his feelings about his ostracism: Cornelius Nepos (Nep. *Them.* 8.2) suggests he lived in Argos in some splendor.

3. *Letters of Themistocles* 8.1; Plut. *Mor.* 605e; Plut. *Vit. Them.* 23.1; Thuc. 1.135.3; Harold Mattingly, "The Practice of Ostracism at Athens," *Antichthon* 25 (1991): 1–26; Sara Forsdyke, *Exile, Ostracism, and Democracy: The Politics of Expulsion in Ancient Greece* (Princeton: Princeton University Press, 2005), 155. Diod. Sic. (11.55.4–8) suggests that Themistocles' ostracism, flight to Argos, condemnation for treason, and his flight to northwest Greece all happened in the same year, 471/0. But most scholars accept that the timeline needs to be stretched out a little, with his exile happening in 471/0, and his condemnation for treason (and his flight from Argos to northwest Greece) around 468.

4. Another of the later *Letters of Themistocles* (4) is written from the perspective of Themistocles' time in Corcyra concerning the fate of his wife and children back Athens. For the Corcyrean reaction see *Letters of Themistocles* 20.

5. See Thuc. 1.136–137; Plut. *Vit. Them.* 24.2–5, 24.6 (family brought to Epirus); Diod. Sic. 11.56.1–6. Also in *Letters of Themistocles* 5.

6. Diod. Sic. 11.56.2.

7. Diod. Sic. 11.56.2–5.

8. Hdt. 7.101. Pausanias recounts that the Delphic Oracle refused gifts from Themistocles after the victory at Salamis (a very unusual occurrence) because the god knew that he would one day become a suppliant of the Persian King: Paus. 10.14.5–6. Other prominent Greeks, including Alcibiades, would, in later times, follow his example of offering their services to Persia. See Athenaeus, *Deipnosophistae* 12.49; Deborah Levine Gera, "Themistocles' Persian Tapestry," *Classical Quarterly* 57, no. 2 (2007): 445–457.

9. See Thuc. 1.137; Plut. *Vit. Them.* 25; Polyaenus, *Strat.* 1.30.8; Nep. *Them.* 8. Plutarch (*Vit. Them.* 25) also records an alternative account of events in which Themistocles attempted first to win the favor of Hieron, the tyrant ruler in Sicily. When this failed, he sailed for Asia. Compare Aeschines of Sphettus, who wrote a dialogue in which Socrates reflects on the highs and lows of Themistocles' career: Aelius Aristides 2.292–294 ("A Reply to Plato").

10. Plut. *Vit. Them.* 25.3. The temple was never completely abandoned; see John Travlos, *Pictorial Dictionary of Ancient Athens* (London: Thames and Hudson, 1971), 121.

11. Plut. *Vit. Them.* 26.1. Diodorus Siculus (11.56–57) relates that Themistocles' contact was named Lysitheides—but the subsequent actions of the man tally with Plutarch's account.

12. Plut. *Vit. Them.* 26.3.

13. For descriptions see Thuc. 1.137.3; Plut *Vit. Them.* 26.3. There is additional description of this journey in the later *Letters of Themistocles* (20.29–30), which also indicates that he learned Persian during his journey.

14. For Thucydides and Plutarch see Richard Stoneman, *Xerxes: A Persian Life* (New Haven: Yale University Press, 2015), 164–180, 202–209; Ctesias, *Persica* 20 (commander accuses the elder son of patricide); Aristotle, *Politics* 5.1311b (commander killed both father and son).

15. For discussion in modern scholarship on this point see Arthur Keaveney, *The Life and Journey of the Athenian Statesman Themistocles (524–460 BCE) as a Refugee in Persia* (Lewiston, N.Y.: Edwin Mellen Press, 2003), 24–25, 102–104, 138–139. There is also a reference in Aristotle ([*Ath. Pol.*] 25.2) to Themistocles' being back in Athens as a supporter of Ephialtes' assault on the Areopagus, which is usually dated to 462 BCE. For discussion of whether Themistocles was able to return to Athens before he left Greece for Persia (as part of a reevaluation of all the key dates of his career and death), see Percy N. Ure, "When Was Themistocles Last in Athens?" *Journal of Hellenic Studies* 41, no. 2 (1921): 165–178; Charles A. Robinson, Jr., "The Date of Themistocles' Ostracism," *American Journal of Philology* 67, no. 3 (1946): 265–266; Arthur. R. Munro, "The Chronology of Themistocles' Career," *Classical Review* 6, no. 8 (1892): 333–334.

16. Thuc. 1.137; see also Nep. *Them.* 10.1; Plut. *Vit. Them.* 28–29. In the later *Letters of Themistocles* (8), the writer expresses his surprise at receiving such a warm welcome given his previous actions against the Persians.

17. Plut. *Vit. Them.* 28–29.

18. This was not without difficulty: Diodorus Siculus recounts that Mandane, the sister of King Xerxes, who had lost four sons at Salamis, came personally to persuade the Persian King to seek vengeance against Themistocles. He initially refused, but she stirred up the nobles and eventually a mob, who rushed the palace demanding vengeance and forcing the King to form a jury of nobles to determine Themistocles' fate. Themistocles defended himself (in Persian) and was acquitted: Diod. Sic. 11.57.

19. Perhaps Themistocles' acquisition of Persian was facilitated by his knowing a language other than Greek from birth, that of his mother, who came from Caria/Thracia, or perhaps he was able to learn it because of his excellent memory (see Quintilian, *Institutes of Oratory* 11.2.50; Valerius Maximus, *Nine Books of Memorable Deeds and* Sayings 8.7 ext. 15). But in the anonymous *Letters of Themistocles* (20.33), the writer claims to have simply absorbed Persian while on his travels. Cornelius Nepos (*Them.* 10.1) indicates that Themistocles eventually spoke Persian like a native. Over forty Greek exiles are known to have come to the Persian court during the Classical period; one of them, Alcibiades, may also have learned Persian, although the report that he did might be a later fiction to make him seem more like Themistocles: Gera, "Themistocles' Persian Tapestry."

20. On his welcome in Persia see Xenophon, *Memorabilia* 3.6.2. On his language skills see Philostratus, *Imagines* 2.31–32, which describes a picture of Themistocles speaking to a crowd; Philostratus is convinced that Themistocles is speaking fluent Persian.

21. Plut. *Vit. Them.* 29.8.

22. Plut. *Vit. Them.* 31.3.

23. See Anthony J. Podlecki, *The Life of Themistocles: A Critical Survey of the Literary and Archaeological Evidence* (Montreal: McGill-Queens University Press, 1975), 169–172; Herbert A. Cahn and Dominique Gerin, "Themistocles at Magnesia," *Numismatic Chronicle* 148 (1988): 13–20; Cahn and Gerin, "Themistocles Again," *Numismatic Chronicle* 151 (1991): 199–202.

24. Plut. *Vit. Them.* 31.1–2.

25. Plut. *Vit. Cim.* 18.5–6 suggests that Cimon aimed to threaten the Persian King's very throne, especially because Themistocles was the King's adviser and had apparently promised to lead a future campaign against Greece.

26. On bull's blood see Aristophanes, *Knights* 83–84; Plut. *Vit. Them.* 31.5–6; Diod. Sic. 11.58.3. See also Plutarch's Life of Flamininus 20.5. Another kind of poison is reported in Thuc. 1.138.4; Plut. *Vit. Cim.* 18.6; Plut. *Vit. Them.* 31.6. Ael. *VH* (9.18) recounts that Themistocles is supposed to have said that when faced with a life choice that leads either to one's death or to an indictment, he would choose death. Diodorus Siculus reports that Themistocles had made the Persian King promise in advance that he and only he would lead an attack on Greece; thus, by killing himself, he forced the King to give up on his ambitions. In this way, Themistocles' suicide is purported to have saved Greece from a new invasion: Diod. Sic. 11.58.1–3. An alternative version of Themistocles' death, preferred by Thucydides and later by Cornelius Nepos, suggests that Themistocles died naturally of an illness: Thuc. 1.138.4; Nep. *Them.* 10.4. For discussion see John Ma, "The Death of Themistocles," *Greece and Rome* 42, no. 2 (1995): 159–167.

27. On Themistocles being treated respectfully by the Persians see Plut. *Vit Them.* 31.7, 32.4; Thuc. 1.138.5; Diod. Sic. 11.58.1. On the promise to incoming Greeks see Plut. *Vit. Them.* 29.9. Equally, the welcome Themistocles received from the Persian King has echoed through time: Napoleon, on his surrender to the British after the Battle of Waterloo in 1815, said that he put himself at the mercy of the British people as Themistocles had done to the Persian King: Royal Collection Trust, Letter of surrender from Napoleon to the Prince Regent, July 13, 1815.

EPILOGUE

1. Plut. *Vit. Them.* 32.4. Cornelius Nepos (*Them.* 10.3) also suggests that the Magnesians put up a statue of Themistocles. See Anthony J. Podlecki, *The Life of Themistocles: A Critical Survey of the Literary and Archaeological Evidence* (Montreal: McGill-Queens University Press, 1975), 43.

2. Thuc. 1.138.6. Pausanias (1.1.2) would later conflate the stories and suggest that Themistocles' bones were brought back to Athens at a later date by his descendants to be buried in a resplendent tomb overlooking the Piraeus.

3. For his sons being welcomed back see Plato, *Meno* 93d–e. The painting in the Parthenon is in Paus. 1.1.2. Pausanias (1.26.4) also tells us that the sons of Themistocles set up a bronze statue of Artemis Leucophryene, the goddess worshipped by the Magnesians, in the Agora at Athens, in thanks for the honor they had shown their

father. The grandson of Themistocles, also called Themistocles, had a prominent tomb along the Sacred Way leading out of Athens: Paus. 1.37.1.

4. See Stesimbrotos, *On Themistocles, Thucydides, and Pericles* (F. Jacoby, *Fragmente der griechischen Historiker* [Berlin: Weidmann, 1923–1959], F1–11); Podlecki, *The Life of Themistocles*, 47–65; Frank J. Frost, "Themistocles' Place in Athenian Politics," *California Studies in Classical Antiquity* 1 (1968): 105–124.

5. See, e.g., Isocrates, 8.75 ("On the Peace").

6. *Supplementum epigraphicum Graecum* XXII.116.5 (praising the 330 BCE refurbishment of the temple); John Travlos, *Pictorial Dictionary of Ancient Athens* (London: Thames and Hudson, 1971), 121. For the hero shrine see Richard E. Wycherley, *The Stones of Athens* (Princeton: Princeton University Press, 1978), 192.

7. Cic., *On Duties* 1.75.

8. Cic., *On Duties* 2.16.

9. Plut. *Mor.* 184f–185c.

Acknowledgments

My sincerest thanks to James Romm, the editor of the Ancient Lives series, for inviting me to participate, and for his guidance and patience throughout the preparation of this volume. I am indebted also to the superb team at Yale University Press, led by Heather Gold, for kind, thoughtful, and professional support; to Susan Laity for her superb copyediting; as well as to Kelsi Russell for her support as a research assistant in the early phases of this project. This book was written through a period of significant change, as my wife and I found new jobs and a new home and welcomed our son, Wilbur, into the world. This book would never have been written among all this upheaval without the incredible support of my wife, Cassie, to whom I am eternally grateful, as well as the support of my wider family, which I hope to be able to return in kind.

This book is dedicated to my infant son, Wilbur, whose journey in life is just beginning. May he always remember that while it is easy to feel that one is surrounded by stories of people who confidently achieve great things and live perfect lives, the reality is much more complex and uncertain – something I hope this book and this series make clear, and thus give heart and encouragement to us all.

Index

Index

Index

Index

Index

Index